How Sweet
The Sound

NOEL DAVIDSON

AMBASSADOR

BELFAST ◆ **GREENVILLE**
NORTHERN IRELAND **SOUTH CAROLINA**

How Sweet The Sound

© Copyright 1997 Noel Davidson

ISBN 1 84030 005 1

AMBASSADOR PRODUCTIONS LTD,
Providence House
16 Hillview Avenue,
Belfast, BT5 6JR
Northern Ireland

Emerald House,
1 Chick Springs Road, Suite 206
Greenville,
South Carolina 29609
United States of America

Contents

❖

Introduction

❖

SOMETIMES, IN LIFE, WE COME ACROSS STRANGE RELATIONSHIPS.

We look at two people, obviously firm friends, and say to ourselves, "Funny friendship that", or, "Surely those two must be like chalk and cheese. How on earth would they ever get on?"

But maybe, you see, we don't know the whole story.

For that's just the way it looked with John and William.

John Newton and William Cowper, that is.

Newton was a strong, forceful, almost domineering character. Always ready to 'give the orders'. William Cowper appeared to be the direct opposite. Shy, nervous, retiring.

On closer examination, however, one would discover that they had a lot in common.

Each had lost his mother before he was eight years old.

Each had been unhappy in childhood.

Each heard the call of God in early life. And trusted in Christ as Saviour.

Both were very clever. And God had a specific use for the talents which He had given to each of them.

So when they were introduced to each other an instant friendship began. Not, as one would suppose and some have suggested, a friendship where one partner dominated the other, like a puppet on a string. It was nothing like that.

It was a relationship founded upon mutual respect.

For twelve years Newton and Cowper lived in the same little town, Olney in Buckinghamshire, and only Newton's responsibilities as curate of the parish ever kept them apart. They spent most of their waking hours in each other's company.

The fruit of that friendship was to provide the Christian world with a lasting legacy. Some of its best-known and most loved hymns. And a hymnbook.

When I was first approached and asked to conduct some research into the life of these two characters, and the hymns which they wrote, it interested me. So I did some reading.

What I discovered, not only interested me. It excited me!

I found, for instance, that hymns like, 'Amazing Grace', 'There is a Fountain Filled with Blood', 'How Sweet the Name of Jesus Sounds', 'Glorious Things of Thee are Spoken', and 'Hark, my Soul, it is the Lord!', all emanated from the wonderful fellowship enjoyed by those two firm friends. And there were more. Hundreds more!

So I began to write.

To obtain all the information necessary to compile this book, I have been a frequent visitor to libraries and antiquarian bookshops. And my wife, Liz, and I, have visited Olney three times. Stopping over to study.

There I was able to sit, lost in thought, in the room where William Cowper wrote, 'God moves in a mysterious way', and walk in the garden where he tended his precious plants, exercised his hares, and communed with his God.

There I visited the church where John Newton preached the Gospel with such sincerity, and the vicarage where he wrote so many beautiful hymns.

Liz and I also spent part of an afternoon just strolling through the meadows where the two men walked and talked together so often, down by the River Ouse.

All this allowed me to get a 'feel' for the lives of these two exceptional hymnwriters. Try to penetrate their thoughts and souls. Discover what 'made them tick', as we sometimes say.

In the period which I have spent in the writing of this book, I have read through the entire Olney Hymn book at least twice, and I have also consulted numerous collections of Cowper's poetical works.

It has been marvellous. A real thrill.

As you read this volume, I trust you will find it instructive. There is just the chance that you may learn a little bit of late eighteenth century history! How much do you know, for example, about pillow lace? Or life on board a sailing ship? Or Bedlam?

And you should also find it interesting.

How the friendship between the two main characters began, and developed. How that William Cowper, despite his frequent bouts of depression, became a famous poet. And how John Newton, the once-upon-a-time blasphemous sea-captain, came to meet the Prime Minister of the day, William Pitt.

Above all, may you find it a blessing.

The title, 'How Sweet The Sound', summarises, for me, the Olney Hymns. They are so varied in style and content. Yet challenging. Comforting. Christ-exalting. In the book, thirty two of the hymns are quoted in full, and with the original wording. Some of them you will recognise straight away. It should be an absorbing exercise to compare them with what we actually sing! Some of them will be totally new to you. As they were to me. Some of William Cowper's spiritual poetry is included, as well. For the literary buffs.

As you read through this book, my most sincere desire is that you may come to know for the first time, or develop a fuller appreciation of, the One who started it all in the first place. The God who saved a rebellious seaman and a budding poet, and used their genial companionship and combined genius to provide us with such a lasting treasure.

The undying Olney Hymns.

Noel I. Davidson
September, 1997.

1

"The Lord Have Mercy On Us"

❖

THINGS WERE LOOKING BLEAK.

The sailing ship 'Greyhound' was plunging through mountainous seas in an Atlantic storm.

John Newton, the twenty-two year old mate was awakened, in the eerie roaring darkness, by a frantic cry from the deck above. "She's sinking! She's sinking!"came the plaintive wail.

As he struggled up towards the deck, battling against sloshing water and floating debris, Newton was horrified to witness the sailor who had been climbing the ladder just ahead of him washed overboard by a monstrous wave.

He was gone forever. Lost. No hope of a rescue in such conditions.

Just after dawn on that morning, 10th March, 1748, Newton was helping some seamen to caulk the tropic-dried timbers of the badly-leaking 'Greyhound'. As they stuffed bits of wood, bedding, and even their own shirts into the cracks in a desperate attempt to stop the inrush of seawater, Newton remarked to a seaman near him, "We are going to have some story to tell over a glass of wine when we go ashore."

The sailor was not impressed. He reckoned that he was finished. This was it. His last storm at sea.

"No," he replied, resignedly, "it is too late now. We cannot save her, or ourselves."

It was now the mate's turn to face the inevitable.

Leaving the seamen to their apparently hopeless task, he went in search of the captain. Having found the master of the vessel, Newton discussed the dire situation with him.

After he had left the captain, and as he battled to make his way back to the pumps across the pitching wave-washed deck, he reflected on their plight.

Then suddenly, almost involuntarily, he said aloud, "If this will not do, the Lord have mercy on us."

He stopped dead, instantly arrested by his own words. "The Lord." He had mentioned "the Lord", and it hadn't been in any blasphemous sense. For the last eight or ten years the only occasions on which he had mentioned the name of the Lord had been in absolute profanity. It hadn't been mere swearing that he had been engaged in, either. Saying "bad words". It had been much deeper, much more sinister than that. It had been studied, deliberate blasphemy against God and all things pertaining to Him.

Now he had spoken the name of the Lord sincerely. Genuinely. Prayerfully almost.

And it had been a cry for mercy!

Could "the Lord have mercy on" them? And particularly on him?

Was there any mercy left in the storehouse of God for the openly rebellious and blatantly blasphemous John Newton?

There must be, for miraculously the waterlogged 'Greyhound' didn't sink. She just kept ploughing on, more in the water than on it, her by-now-exhausted crew manning the pumps, day after day after day.

On March 21st, mate Newton, physically worn out at the pumps, took his turn lashed to the helm on deck. As he stood there, battered by the waves and freezing cold, his whole life passed before him.

He remembered his godly mother who had taught him passages from the Bible as he had stood at her knee, and who had sung some of Dr. Isaac Watts' "Divine Songs for Children" to him at bedtime. She had died when he was still only a child and his father, a sea captain, had arranged for his only son to follow in his seafaring footsteps. From then on it had been downhill all the way.

As the little sailing ship plunged headlong fom crest to trough of wave after wave John Newton recalled the near escapes. There was the time when he nearly died after a flogging for running away from his ship, and the occasion when he was saved from almost certain drowning by his shipmates when he, who couldn't swim, was about to jump overboard after a drunken revelry. And there were many more besides...

Could there be a merciful God somewhere who had His mighty hand on him? In spite of the open vociferous opposition? Despite the awful blasphemy?

John Newton was struggling with the helm of the 'Greyhound' as he tried to head the battered little vessel into the wind. He was wrestling with more than the helm, however. Reflection on days and years gone past had stirred up a storm of conviction in his soul.

Some portions of Scripture which he had learnt in earlier life flashed across his mind with remarkable clarity. To the accompaniment of roaring wind and crashing waves he repeated aloud Proverbs 1 vs. 24 - 31 :-

> *"Because I have called, and ye refused; I have stretched out my hand, and no man regarded;*
> *But ye have set at nought all my counsel, and would none of my reproof :*
> *I also will laugh at your calamity; I will mock when your fear cometh ;*
> *When your fear cometh as desolation, and your destruction cometh as a whirlwind; when distress and anguish cometh upon you.*
> *Then shall they call upon me, but I will not answer; they shall seek me early, but they shall not find me :*
> *For that they hated knowledge, and did not choose the fear of the Lord :*
> *They would none of my counsel: they despised all my reproof.*
> *Therefore shall they eat of the fruit of their own way, and be filled with their own devices."*

That was him summed up. Newton in a nutshell.

He resolved that if the storm abated, and he was spared, he would take some time and study the New Testament in the cabin. Could God still have mercy?

The storm did abate and when the sailors began to take stock of their situation they found that there was some good news. And some bad. The good news was that the "Greyhound" was almost free of water. A few more hours on the pumps would clear her completely. The bad news was that at the height of the storm most of the livestock which had been kept to provide food, the pigs, sheep and poultry, had been washed overboard. All they had left to live on until they reached port were a few casks of salted cod. Enough food for one week, if strictly rationed. And definitely no more than a week.

When he was afforded time off from working on the pumps in the days that followed, John Newton fulfilled his resolve. He began to study the New Testament, beginning with the Gospels. He was desperately seeking peace of mind.

While perusing the Gospel of Luke one evening the words of chapter 11 v.3 arrested his attention :-

"If ye then, being evil, know how to give good gifts to your children : how much more shall your heavenly Father give the Holy Spirit to them that ask him?"

God would give the Holy Spirit to them that asked Him, it said. Newton reasoned that if he prayed for help and light God would give it to him.

And he was right. God did.

As the physically weary, but spiritually awakened mariner sat in that sodden cabin he began to realise that there was forgiveness for him. He was drawn in spirit to the cross of Christ. Perhaps he remembered the words of Dr. Watts' hymn which his mother had taught him :-

"When I survey the wondrous cross,
On which the Prince of Glory died..."

John Newton discovered that in the death of Christ at Calvary he could find forgiveness for all his sins. However many or however heinous. Christ had borne the judgment of God for the sin of the world. That included sceptical, scornful seamen.

His experience of conversion is best summarised by himself in a hymn he wrote years later, entitled, "Looking at the Cross."

In evil long I took delight,
Unawed by shame or fear;
Till a new object struck my sight,
And stopped my wild career.

I saw one hanging on a tree,
In agonies and blood;
Who fixed his languid eyes on me,
As near his cross I stood.

Sure, never till my latest breath,
Can I forget that look;
It seemed to charge me with his death,
Though not a word he spoke.

My conscience felt, and owned my guilt,
And plunged me in despair;
I saw my sins his blood had spilt,
And helped to nail him there.

Alas! I knew not what I did,
But now my tears are vain;
Where shall my trembling soul be hid?
For I the LORD have slain.

A second look he gave, which said,
"I freely all forgive;
This blood is for thy ransom paid,
I die that thou may'st live."

Thus, while his death my sin displays,
In all its blackest hue;
(Such is the mystery of grace)
It seals my pardon too.

With pleasing grief and mournful joy,
My spirit now is filled;
That I should such a life destroy,
Yet live by him I killed.
(Olney Hymns. Book 2. Hymn57.)

Two significant changes occured in the life of Newton after he had seen "one hanging one a tree". One was a stop. The other a start. He stopped blaspheming. The man who had sworn so flagrantly never uttered another oath. And he started praying. His early stumbling prayers were neither as long or as fluent as those of his later days, but they were extremely sincere. They were spontaneous outbursts of a grateful soul. He praised God for his deliverance from the storm which had held him in fear for days and the sin which had held him in bondage for years, and he prayed specifically for two things. That he would learn more about God and His ways and will, and that they would reach port safely so that he could tell his father, and Mary, his childhood sweetheart, of his marvellous experiences.

There were other obstacles to be overcome, however. Conditions on board ship became more difficult by the day. The food was almost finished. Half a salted cod was divided amongst all twelve crew members each day. That was their ration. They were all extremely weak and inadequately clothed for the bitterly cold weather.

To complicate matters for Newton, the captain then decided that all the ship's misfortunes had come about because they had a Jonah on board. Him. God was pouring out judgment upon them because of Newton's reckless earlier life, he reckoned.

Whilst to a certain extent understanding the logic of the captain's argument, the alleged "Jonah" also knew something of the fate of that enigmatic Bible character. He recognised that this idea, if accepted by the other crew members, could have serious implications for him. So he took to staying in his cabin when off duty. Praying and reading the New Testament.

On April 7th, to everyone's absolute delight, the shout of "Land Ahoy!" rang out from the look-out , and the next day the 'Greyhound' limped up Lough Swilly on the north-west coast of Ireland. They were safe, at last!

As soon as they possibly could, most of the crew rushed ashore to the nearest inn for some "refreshment". His fellow-sailors were astounded that Newton chose to stay on board, rather than joining them in their celebration.

So it was that the sailor who thought he would never taste another glass of wine was ashore having one, and recounting his adventures to all who would listen! Meanwhile John Newton, who had suggested such an activity in the first place, remained in his cabin reading a book of sermons which he had found, and the New Testament. And praying to his God. Amazing grace!

2

Tongue-Tied

❖

WHEN JOHN NEWTON EVENTUALLY WENT ASHORE
AT LONDONDERRY, HE DID TWO THINGS.

The first was that he wrote, and dispatched, two letters.
One of these was to his father, who had long since given his
sea-faring son up for dead. Just to let him know that John
junior was still alive, considerably changed, and homeward
bound.The second letter was to an aunt of Mary Catlett, the
girl he had met in his early teenage, and whose memory he
could never erase from his hyper-active brain. It was more
than a mere request for information, though. It was a plea
from the heart. How was Mary? And more importantly, was
she still unmarried? If so, would she ever, possibly, still be
interested in him? "A poor sailor returning from the sea after
many heart-rending trials." Oh, what agony! Replies to both
letters to be sent to Liverpool, where he hoped to arrive soon
after the 'Greyhound' was declared sea-worthy again.

His second decisive action was to go to Church. John Newton, who hadn't been inside a church door since his mother took him to the "dissenting chapels" as a child, sought out and went to a place of worship. This action caused consternation amongst his mocking mates. Newton at church! Unbelievable!

As he sat in church for the first time in years, John Newton was overwhelmed. How kind and patient God had been. Preserving him, confronting him, saving him... He pledged himself that day to live for ever in the service of God.

Recounting his Londonderry experience to someone, years later, he said, "It was then that I learnt to appreciate the obedience of Jesus Christ. I embraced the sublime doctrine of God manifest in flesh, reconciling the world to Himself."

In late May, his ship was sufficiently repaired to return to her home port of Liverpool. Sailing down the Irish Sea, he thought often of the letters. What kind of replies, if any, awaited him?

After helping to secure the ship, Newton went in search of his much-anticipated mail, only to find that there was just one letter for him. From his father. John Newton, senior, was delighted that his son was still alive and well, and noted that he was still affectionately interested in Mary Catlett.

The big blow, the horrible deflation of that affection, however, came in the fact that there was no letter from Mary's aunt. No news whatsoever about her.

Had he missed her after all? Was she married to someone else?

Unthinkable.

But what was he to do?

In despondent mood he sat down and wrote again. Pleading for news of some sort, for it would be easier to live with knowing something, than knowing nothing, he assured Mary's aunt :-

"I am determined from this moment to divert my thoughts from her, as much as possible, and tho I do not expect to ever be able to wholly conquer my passion, I will endeavour to keep it within my own breast, and never trouble either her, or you, any more with it...."

Having thus poured out the feelings of his breaking heart the young Newton was compelled to consider other matters. And one of these was employment. What was he going to do with himself? A Christian now, but whose only experience was the rugged life of a seafarer...

Joseph Manesty, a ship-owner in Liverpool, knew John Newton, and recognised in him exceptional qualities of leadership. So he offered the twenty-three year old a job. As captain of a slave ship.

After considering this prospect of promotion for a while the young seaman turned it down. Not for any moral scruples as yet, but because he did not consider himself sufficiently experienced to become a captain. Not in the meantime, anyway.

Then came a shaft of daylight in the gloom of uncertainty that had surrounded him since his return to Liverpool. It was a letter from Mary's aunt.

The news was, at the very least, hopeful.

Mary was well, a lively and attractive young woman of nineteen, and as yet unmarried. That same letter contained another totally unexpected, but mightily encouraging, item of news. His father, before embarking on another voyage, had visited the Catlett home in Chatham and given his consent to any union of the two of them, "should matters progress."

Now John Newton had something more to live for! He immediately hired a horse, rode to Warrington, and caught the next coach to the south. He was in London in four days.

Rather nervously, he went to visit the Catletts. George Catlett, father, received him courteously. Mary's mother received him inquisitively. She had all sorts of questions about his life at sea, his present state of health, and his future plans.

But what about the one that really mattered? Mary. How would she receive him?

When his big moment came, the moment he had been almost too scared to contemplate whilst at sea, in case it would never come to pass, the totally awestruck Newton let himself down frightfully. When John Newton, worldly-wise far beyond his years, was left alone with the girl of his dreams, the beautiful Mary, he completely seized up. Became hopelessly tongue-tied! Couldn't utter a single word!

When, at last, he did compose himself sufficiently to say something, it was only to ask Mary if he could write her a letter!

Very graciously, but doubtless with some degree of amazement, or perhaps amusement, she consented.

So embarrassed was the young suitor with his performace that he walked all the way back to Liverpool. From London! It took him weeks!

During an overnight inn-stop on the way he wrote the promised letter, expressing his love very tenderly, and asking Mary if she could possibly, "bestow a little of your Charity upon me".

On arriving back in Liverpool, he discovered that Joseph Manesty had a different job to offer him. Mate on board a slaveship, 'The Brownlow'.

John Newton accepted this position, and went to sea again. As well as earning a pound or two, it would allow him breathing space. Thinking-about-Mary time.

He was not long back into his old environment until he was back into his old ways. It had been relatively simple to be a Christian ashore. But being aboard was different. Satan wasn't going to let him have it too easy.

Telling of that struggle, Newton confessed :-

"The enemy prepared a train of temptations, and I became an easy prey. For about a month he lulled me to sleep in a course of evil, of which, a few months   before, I could not have supposed myself any longer capable."

However, when Satan attacked, God counter-attacked.

Newton was struck down with a violent fever. He became so ill that he was convinced that he was going to die. This was it.

Absolutely drained and exhausted he cast himself down on a beach in Sierra Leone, West Africa. It was then that God spoke to him. Forcefully. Powerfully.

Fifteen years later, he described that beach experience to a friend in a letter, thus:-

"Here I found a renewed liberty to pray. I durst make no more resolves but cast myself before the Lord, to do with me as He should please. From that time I have been delivered from the power and domination of sin... It was the powerful grace of God which delivered me from any further such black declensions."

Immediately upon returning from that voyage, a stronger Christian, John Newton proceeded with all speed to Chatham. He had a piece of important business to which he must attend. He was going to propose to Mary. And he was determined not to make such an ass of himself this time! He had rehearsed what he was going to say, in the lime groves of Africa, in the loneliness of his cabin, or during the long night watches at the helm...

When the long-awaited opportunity presented itself, however, it was more of the same! Tongue-tied again! The seaman who was so literate that he could compose poems about Mary with apparent ease and who could write flowing letters, found it difficult to express his much-practised proposal in words when it came to the bit!

The tick of the big grandfather clock in the corner cracked open the silence.

Eventually, he did manage to stumble out his proposal, though not as fluently as he would have liked. And Mary refused.

Not to be deterred, he repeated his proposal an hour or so later. And she still refused.

Driven by desperation, he became much more articulate, and proposed again.

This time Mary accepted. She loved the jittery seaman just as much as he loved her. But she had no intention of letting him know that! Not for a while, at least.

So on February 1st, 1750, John Newton, aged twenty-four, and Mary Catlett, aged twenty-one, were married in St. Margaret's Church, in Rochester, Kent, England.

This happy occasion was to prove a most important turning-point in the life of the mariner.

Only one event in his life was more outstanding.

That was his conversion to God in an Atlantic storm.

3

A Genteel Occupation?

❖

HAPPILY MARRIED, SHORT OF MONEY, AND UN-EMPLOYED.

Such was the situation that John Newton found himself in during the summer of 1750. He was blissfully content with Mary, but he knew that he needed some means of support for the both of them. In short, he needed a job.

But what could he do? His whole working life until that moment had been spent at sea. Braving mighty waves with rough companions in tiny ships. It was all he knew. So he went back to it.

Joseph Manesty contacted him again, with another offer of promotion. To Captain. And Newton accepted.

That first parting with Mary was a heart-breaking affair. They both agreed that it was "bitter as death." Mary was worried about the many obvious hardships looming up ahead for her new husband, not least of which was a very immediate one. "Beware of highwaymen", she cautioned, "and don't be riding the English roads after dark!"

John felt guilty at leaving her, but there was no alternative. It had to be done.

And it was.

After praying aloud together in the house, they walked out to the waiting horse. When he had mounted, John Newton leaned down, kissed his wife, then rode off. He couldn't bear to look back.

Captain John Newton had an interest in, and a flair for, writing. So he decided to keep a detailed log of his voyage.

Procuring a new leather-bound foolscap book he inscribed the first page:-

> *Journal kept on board the Duke of Argyle*
> *from Liverpool to Africa*
> *Commenced ye 14th August 1750.*
>
> *They that go down to the sea in ships, that do business in*
> *great waters;*
> *These see the works of the Lord, and his wonders in the*
> *deep.*

This was one of the first logs ever kept of a voyage of a slave-ship, and it certainly was the first one to include a Scripture reference!

The first entry in that log reads, "Cast from the pier at Liverpool."

And little did John Newton know of what lay before him.

The crew threatened to mutiny on a number of occasions. When they went ashore in West Africa some of them became so drunk that they had to be located and dragged back aboard.

During the dangerous Middle Passage, from Africa to America, twenty of the slaves broke free from their irons and threatened to overpower the crew. Then they attempted to poison the precious drinking water.

'The Duke of Argyle' wasn't proving to be an easy first command for Captain Newton (junior)!

But why was he involved in such an occupation at all? A Christian, captain of a slave-ship?

It must be remembered that in the mid-eighteenth century, to be a sea-captain of any sort was considered a noble and profitable career. A "genteel occupation."

And gradually John Newton introduced changes on board his ship.

He conducted a service for the crew every Sunday. His first services consisted of readings from the Book of Common Prayer. But as he grew in confidence and in the knowledge of Christian things he soon discovered that, "The Book of Common prayer is unsuitable for congregations such as mine who are for ye most part the refuse and dregs of ye nation."

So he adapted! He devised a form of service more appropriate to his "congregation". Useful practice for years to come!

He also ensured that the necessary punishments meted out on board his ship were not nearly as brutal as those on board other vessels, and he protected the female slaves from the abuse that was common at the time.

On earlier voyages Newton had satisfied his quest for knowledge by reading extensively in the Latin classics and poring over the first four books of Euclid. Now he had an added reading interest. His Bible. Many off-duty hours he spent reading and trying to understand Scriptural truths that were totally new to him.

And he spent hours in prayer. Asking God for His help and protection.

In addition to prayer and a wide variety of reading, Newton's other pastime aboard was writing to, and thinking about, Mary. He wrote to her almost every day. These letters he dispatched in bundles on reaching the next port.

On clear evenings he stood on deck and gazed in wonder at the canopy of the heavens. And thought of Mary. Before he sailed, he and his new wife had agreed that at a certain hour each week, they would each look towards the north star. This simple act bound their hearts together in love, though thousands of miles of ocean separated them.

When the slave ships were moored side by side in the West Indies, John Newton endured much good-natured mocking and raillery from his fellow captains as they sat to exchange tales of the sea in the evenings. They just failed to understand a sea-captain who prayed to God, read his Bible and wrote letters to his wife!

After completing his first, largely successful, voyage as a captain, John Newton arrived back in Liverpool on 8 th October, 1751, and in early November he was with his much-missed Mary again. They had a lot to talk about. And had the winter to do it.

During those months ashore Newton became acquainted with two books which had just recently been published. He purchased a copy of each of them, and they were to prove invaluable to him on his next voyage.

Joseph Manesty had been so pleased with his young captain's first command that he put him in charge of a brand new ship, 'The African', and in it Captain Newton set sail for the second time in June 1752.

During the long hours at sea he threw himself into a regular routine of study, exercise and prayer. Rising early he read the Bible for two hours. Then, after spending another hour or two reading Latin or studying mathematics, he engaged in exercise. Walking on deck. Midday was prayer time.

John Newton's spiritual appetite began to increase. Reading Latin verse and studying the geometry of Euclid were excellent means of keeping the alert mind sharp, but they did not contribute to spiritual growth. It was in this realm that the two books which he had purchased when ashore proved so valuable to him.

In the solitude of his cabin, when freed from the seemingly endless round of responsibility, Newton read these volumes over and over again. Both had been written by Philip Doddridge, a dissenting minister from Northampton, and an accomplished hymn-writer.

The first was a biography. And a testimony. 'The Life of Colonel James Gardiner', told the story of how the fast-living Colonel was convicted, then saved, by the power of God. Colonel Gardiner died in the Battle of Prestonpans, in 1745. Newton enjoyed this book. He was greatly moved by it for it seemed like a mirror image of his own experience.

The other book was a more practical volume. Entitled, 'The Rise and Progress of Religion in the Soul', it charted the development of a Christian life. Beginning with, "The careless sinner awakened", it went on to address such matters as, "The established Christian urged to usefulness".

The perusal of this particular book both enlightened, and challenged the thoughtful captain. So much so that he determined to conduct his "Sea-Sunday in a more meaningful manner."

These books, along with his Bible, provided a source of solace and reflection for the captain. And he needed it.

Life aboard was far from easy.

When they stopped at West Africa to take on a fresh cargo of slaves, four of the crew members contracted fever, and died.

Newton then discovered that another crew member, when ashore, had been stirring up his mates to start a mutiny. Dealing with these problems, as a changed man, a Christian man, took great grace. And wisdom. And restraint.

During the dreaded Middle Passage further unrest broke out amongst the already depleted and thus overworked crew. And then amongst the cargo. The slaves. More complications to cope with. Captain Newton consoled himself with the fact that at least when he reached the West Indies there would be a pile of letters waiting for him from Mary. They would cheer him up.

Alas, a big disappointment was in store. A sickening anti-climax to the high expectation which had sustained him through difficult days at sea.

When 'The African' anchored in the harbour at Basseterre on the island of St. Christopher there was no mail for Captain John Newton. Not one single letter. Not one single loving word from his beloved Mary.

Something serious must be wrong. There was something badly amiss.

Mary always wrote him long and detailed letters.

Five days later a ship arrived from England. But still no letters from Mary.

The anxious husband committed his wife and the whole letter-matter to God in prayer. Perhaps the letters had gone astray somehow. Or perhaps, could it just be, that something had happened to her...?

After a tense nine-day wait, another ship arrived from England with letters. But there were none from Mary.

There could only be one answer to this deafening silence from home. Despite the efforts of the other captains in the harbour, who concocted all sorts of ideas to try to persuade him otherwise, John Newton convinced himself that there was only one logical conclusion to the whole affair.

Mary must be dead.

Imagine his great delight then, when two days later, a ship arrived from Antigua, another island, carrying six letters from Mary! They had simply been misdirected. What a relief!

While the ship's captain was worrying about his Mary, work had been progressing. The cargo of slaves had been brought ashore and the holds had been refilled with sugar, cotton and rum.

In August 1753, Captain Newton arrived back in Liverpool, after his second round trip in charge, to a second happy reunion with Mary.

After a pleasant seven week period spent with his wife in lodgings in Liverpool, John Newton sailed again for West Africa. By now, however, he was beginning to become rather disillusiond with the seafaring way of life. He hated the partings from Mary, and he was becoming uneasy "in an employment that was perpetually conversant with chains, bolts and shackles", as he described it himself.

It was while moored in Basseterre harbour on this third voyage that Newton met someone who was to be used of God to lead him deeper into spiritual things.

His name was Alex Clunie. He too was a captain, but he was not engaged in the slave trade. And he was a sincere well-read Christian.

Although Captain Clunie was ten years older than Newton the two men struck up an instant friendship. They had so much in common. Their love for the Lord. Their interest in the study of the Bible. Their working knowledge of the sea, and ships.

After the day's work was done, in the gentle warmth of the evening, these two men spent hours together, studying the Scriptures. Sometimes in Captain Newton's cabin, sometimes in Captain Clunie's, as the clamour of the harbour continued outside, the older man unveiled to his eager friend some of the wonders of the Word.

From Captain Clunie, John Newton learnt of the eternal security of the believer. Up until this point he had been afraid of himself. He had been scared that with the manifold temptations around him he might lapse. Slip back into his old sinful ways. And God would reject him forever. What a thrill it was for him to discover that, "I can expect to be preserved, not by my own power and holiness, but by the mighty power and promise of God through faith in an unchangeable Saviour."

He learnt many other precious lessons, too, in those tropical-evening Bible studies. He learnt more about prayer. And praying. The abiding presence of his Saviour by his side became a practical reality. Until he met Captain Clunie, John Newton had imagined his God as being some sort of very distant Mighty Power who had condescended to show him mercy. But Someone who was far away, and unapproachable.

It was thrilling to realize that the Lord was with him, beside him, through every day and in every situation. "Lo, I am with you alway," He had said. And He meant it.

Before leaving the island of St. Kitts, John Newton's witnessing to others had become more confident, his praying to God had become more earnest, and his reading of the Bible had become more relevant.

On 20th June, 1754, John Newton bade farewell to his friend, and spiritual mentor, Alex. Clunie, and set sail for home.

As he sailed up the Mersey to his home port of Liverpool, seven weeks later, Captain Newton was a more complete Christian. His Heavenly Captain had taught him many things. Important things. Preparatory things.

He was about to set the compass of His servant's life in a completely different direction. A totally different kind of experience lay in store.

John Newton would never go to sea again.

4

'The Business Of Heaven'

❖

MARY NEWTON AND HER HUSBAND SAT CHATTING
ANIMATEDLY IN THE PARLOUR OF THE MANESTY'S
LIVERPOOL HOME. THEY WANTED TO SAY AS MUCH
AS THEY COULD TO EACH OTHER. TIME WAS RUN-
NING OUT FOR THEM. IMPENDING SEPARATION
LOOMED LARGE ONCE MORE.

It was November 1754, and John Newton was due to
return, albeit more reluctantly than ever, to sea again, in two
days time, as captain of 'The Bee.' A new, and hopefully faster,
vessel, than either of his two previous commands.

Then something unusual happened.

God intervened. Dramatically.

John had a fit. "Of ye Apoplectic kind."

Rising from his chair, he placed a hand up to his forehead,
and then collapsed to the floor. He lay there, motionless.

Mary called out for help.

Their hosts and a number of servants, recognising the note of urgency in Mary's cry, came bustling in.

A physician was summoned, in haste.

For almost an hour, Newton lay on the floor. Alive, but only just, it seemed.

Then he opened his eyes. And began to recover. After being helped up onto the sofa, he complained of being very shaky and very dizzy.

He was put to bed.

His subsequent recovery was remarkable.

Two days later, he was well enough to stand by the Customs House and watch "The Bee" set sail for Africa with a hurriedly apppointed new captain.

The doctors had declared him unfit for the rigours of the sea. God had so ordered the circumstances of his life that John Newton was finished with the Slave Trade, as a sea-going captain.

Mary and he returned to Chatham. To reflect. And recuperate.

During the ensuing winter and spring months, spent in Kent, Newton had two deeply enriching, but totally different, types of spiritual experience.

He cultivated the habit of walking, and worshipping, alone. Out in the fields with God. In his diary at the time he described, "morning devotions in ye fields, in ye great temple which the Lord has built for His own."

The other experience was in direct contrast to solitary communion with God in the Kent countryside. It was attending vast gatherings in London, early in the morning, to hear a powerful preacher. His name was George Whitefield.

Evangelical revival was sweeping across England. People were flocking, in their thousands, to hear the Word of God. John Newton was one of them.

Rising very early, he made his way, over dark and dangerous roads, to Moorfields in the capital, to hear Whitefield preach.

Recounting those early morning events to an audience, years later, he said, "Many were the winter mornings when I got up at four to attend Whitefield's tabernacle discourses at five. I have seen Moorfields as full of lanthorns at these times as, I suppose, the Haymarket is full of flambeaux on an opera night."

A diary entry for a Sunday during that winter of spiritual instruction graphically describes the crowds, the atmosphere, and the effect upon the converted captain, of those gatherings:-

"Rose at 4 and after private prayer went to ye Tabernacle, was admitted upon producing ye ticket and here indeed I had a blessing: there were about 1000 or more people of different persuasions but all agreed in ye great essentials of ye Gospel and in mutual charity, worshipping the Lord with one heart and soul. Never before had I such an idea and foretaste of ye business of heaven ... we were about 3 hours in ye ordinance, at the end I went away rejoicing."

Newton read all the published works of both Whitefield and John Wesley, who was also attracting large crowds wherever he preached. These works led him to "adore the free grace of God", in both of them.

The understanding which John Newton developed in those spiritually formative winter-into-spring months at Chatham led him to another conclusion. Captain Clunie had been right. He should be telling others of his faith. He wrote in his diary, "Of late I have had my mouth something opened... and am ashamed to think how long I hid my talent."

Although he greatly enjoyed the freedom to read in Latin and Greek at leisure, to ramble in the countryside, and attend the many meetings in the capital, more practical considerations began to occupy the fertile mind of the ex-sea-captain during the early summer of 1755. He was almost thirty years of age, had a wife to suppport, and was out of work. He needed a job. Again. And it had to be ashore, this time.

Mr. Manesty came to the rescue, once more. On hearing that a position had become vacant for a Tide Surveyor in the Customs office at the port of Liverpool, he recommended John Newton for the job. And with the former captain's in-depth knowledge of ships and sailors, he was appointed.

In August, he signed a contract in London, and was required to set out immediately to take up his new position in Liverpool. To his deep dismay, however, he had to leave Mary behind. Following his fit, Mary had become quite ill and was still much too weak to travel. So John Newton, happy to have work to go to, but sad to have to leave Mary to go to it, set out to take up his new employment. Alone.

A few days after commencing his new job, Tide Surveyor Newton described his duties and working environment, in a letter to Mary :-

> *"I find my duty is to attend the tides one week, and to visit the ships that arrive, and such as are in the river ; and the other week to inspect the vessels in the docks, and thus alternately the year round. The latter is little more than a sinecure, but the former requires pretty constant attendance, both by day and night. I have a good office, with fire and candle, fifty or sixty people under my direction, with a handsome six-oared boat and a coxswain, to row me about..."*

The Tide Surveyors were, in fact, customs officers, employed to search incoming vessels for contraband. Illegally imported goods such as rum, brandy, tobacco, and coffee could fetch high prices on the black market. A perk of the job was that half of the value of any seizure was awarded to the successful Surveyor, as a bonus. This newly found source of additional income led Newton to write in his diary:-

> *"began to reap some of the profits of my new office and to my grief and surprise found too much of the love of money, which is the root of all evil, spring up in my heart..."* !

Despite his misgivings, it was work, satisfying work, for which his early experiences had left him marvellously qualified. He was reasonably happy in it.

He was even happier, though, that his off-duty periods allowed him to diligently pursue his Christian interests. And much to his great delight, George Whitefield visited Liverpool in September, 1755, to preach at a number of open-air gatherings. Newton was thrilled to hear him address a crowd of almost four thousand people one Sunday afternoon in St. Thomas's Square.

This time the by-now well-read and beginning-to-witness-boldly believer wasn't going to hang back. He wanted to identify himself with the man of God. And he did.

The famous evangelist and the Christian customs-man became firm friends.

Whitefield's eloquent and earnest preaching, and sincere personal encouragement, inspired John. It was this influence that turned the thoughts of the occasionally-tongue-tied-ex-captain towards a life in some sort of a preaching ministry. Where, or to whom, he didn't know yet. But the idea had been sown in his mind.

Another thrilling moment for the Liverpool Tide Surveyor was when he received a very special letter from Mary, who was still recovering in Chatham. In it she informed her anxious, but absent, husband, "I have prayed from the heart for the first time. I have called upon God and He has delivered me." Mary had been struggling along beside an increasingly on-fire-for-God husband, becoming ever more discontent with the formalism of her own religion.

Now she too had entered into a deep personal experience with God.

How husband John rejoiced!

God had intervened in his wife's life also. Now they could go forward in life, and in faith, together. That was, of course, if only they could be together.

But they were still almost two hundred and fifty miles apart! That, too, was all set to change.

In October, 1755, Mary's doctor pronounced her fit enough to undertake the long and arduous coach journey to Liverpool. On hearing this news, John was again overjoyed. So delighted was he indeed, that he couldn't wait for her to make the whole northward journey alone. Boarding a south-bound coach he set out to meet his dear Mary halfway. After difficult journeys in unsprung coaches over horrendous roads in different directions, the pair eventually met up at Stone, in Staffordshire. In a coaching-inn called , 'The Bull and Bear.'

Oh the wonder of that reunion! They were now united, not only by a deep love for one another, but also by a deep love for their Lord.

There was so much to talk about. And to plan.

As they waited to catch the next Liverpool-bound coach they reviewed their lives together, to date, recognising the guiding hand of God at every turn. And they made some resolutions for the future.

John and Mary determined, jointly,"to declare God's goodness together, not merely in secret or to each other, but by the whole course of our lives ; to love Him more than we love each other ; and to commit to Him our dearest concerns, and in every trouble to go to Him who has so often heard our prayers and done us good."

A sound basis, surely, for lives to be spent together in the service of God.

They had made remarkable progress in "ye business of heaven".

5

'Appointed For Sanctuary Service'

❖

THE SEVEN YEARS WAR WITH FRANCE, WHICH
BROKE OUT IN AUGUST 1756, WAS BAD NEWS FOR
ENGLAND AND MANY ENGLISH SEAMEN, BUT IT WAS
GOOD NEWS FOR TIDE SURVEYORS.

Press-gangs roamed the streets of major cities again, and
young men were conscripted unceremoniously into the Navy.
Almost half of the ships that sailed from the port of Liverpool
never returned. Many lives were lost.

With a high percentage of the nation's shipping engaged
in fighting a war at sea, the amount of commerce passing
through the ports was greatly reduced. So too was the level of
smuggling.

The consequently diminished work-load for Tide Surveyor
Newton allowed him more off-duty periods in which to pursue his ever-more-time-consuming Christian interests. And
he used it profitably.

With more time to spend at home during the day, John began to hold regular family devotions, attended by Mary, their servants, and any visiting friends. This "expounding the Scriptures in my own family", as he described it, did not come easily to him. His first attempts were self-conscious, stilted and slow, but he persisted. Gradually, and as he grew in confidence, these "expositions" became expected and esteemed elements in the Newton household routine.

During his periods of leave, which because of the continuation of the war began to increase both in frequency and in length, John took Mary on a number of visits to Yorkshire where the evangelical revival was in full swing. It was on these visits that they witnessed at first hand the mighty power of God to save souls and transform lives, in great numbers. And it was in these gatherings, some of which were in remote rural areas, that John Newton began to speak with any confidence in public.

He began by telling his life story. Giving his testimony. Recounting God's marvellous dealings in grace with him.

This story, told with such feeling, and many nautical and natural illustrations, became popular with audiences. People flocked to hear the converted slave-trader recount his experiences in graphic detail.

As he became more self-assured, Newton progressed from retelling his life-story to preaching the Gospel and expounding the Scriptures. As God began to bless his ministry he began to feel increasingly that this was how he wanted to spend the rest of his life.

This was confirmed to him by a number of his Yorkshire friends, both from the dissenting and established church communities, who approached him on various occasions, early in 1758, proposing that he take holy orders. Become a full-time minister of the Gospel.

The prospect of it appealed to him. But there were a number of practical questions to be answered. A number of down-to-earth issues to be considered.

How, for instance, would Mary take to it?

And realistically, could they live on it? He had an excellent job as a Tide Surveyor. Good pay and conditions. And very little hassle these days. Would he be wise to leave all that behind?

Minister's stipends were not reputed to be overly generous.

There again, what about himself? A self-taught ex-seaman whom God had arrested in his wild career, and saved by His grace. Would anybody really want him?

And could he do the job, even if anybody did?

He needed to come to some sort of a conclusion about the matter, one way or another. And he set aside a special day to do just that.

It was his thirty-third birthday, in the summer of 1758.

He spent that day in prayer and fasting. Alone with God from six o'clock in the morning until almost five in the late afternoon. And by that time he had his answer.

His diary entry for that day leaves no doubt what it was :-

"From this time I only wait for light and direction, when and where to move and to begin...I pray I may be enabled to wait patiently, till I clearly see the Lord going before me, and making me a plain path. But in my own mind I already consider myself as torn off from the world and worldly concerns, and devoted and appointed for sanctuary service."

With his mind thus settled John Newton's big problem was the "when and where to move and to begin". Where did he start ?

Having given the matter due consideration, and having considered that he could reach more people with the Gospel through the established church, he applied for ordination in the Church of England. And was refused. On a number of occasions.

The Bishops were not keen to ordain a man who was known to "mix with methodists". And someone who didn't have a University education.

This so-called lack of education as an excuse, disgusted John Wesley, who at that time still considered himself a good Anglican. He wrote in his diary on the 20th March, 1760 :-

> *"I had a good deal of conversation with Mr. Newton. His case is very peculiar. Our church requires that clergymen should be men of learning, and, to this end, have a University education. But how many have a University education and yet no learning at all! Yet these men are ordained. Meantime, one of eminent learning, as well as unblameable behaviour, cannot be ordained because he was not at the University! What a mere farce is this! Who would believe that any Christian bishop would stoop to so poor an evasion?"*

Somewhat disappointed at the reticence of the Church of England to ordain him to the ministry, and having been granted extended leave from his by-now-very-slack job as Tide Surveyor, John Newton accepted an invitation from the Congregational Church in Warwick to fill a temporary vacancy there. It was for three months during the summer of 1760.

Leaving Mary at Chatham, he travelled to Warwick with keen anticipation. This was to be his first church-based steady period of ministry. Walking in the fields one day communing with God, as was his habit, he obtained great reassurance when he recalled the Lord's encouragement to Paul in Acts 18, "Fear not... for I have much people in this city."

Reflecting on his Warwick experiences to a friend, some time later, he remarked, with a twinkle in his eye, "I was afterwards disappointed to discover that Paul was not John, and Corinth was not Warwick!"

He was learning practical lessons in the school of God!

Being still convinced that the Church of England was the place where God would have him engage in full-time ministry, John Newton declined to accept the invitation of the Warwick Church to become their minister, and continued to work as Tide Surveyor in Liverpool. And he endeavoured to "wait patiently".

To pass the long days of waiting, and to express his Christian beliefs and aspirations through a different medium, John turned to writing.

He put it all down on paper.

First of these writings were a series of six sermons. They were intended as samples of the type of sermon that he would have preached. That is, if he had anywhere to preach them!

When his sermons were published, but as yet unpreached, the converted slave captain began a series of eight letters, recounting God's marvellous dealings in his life.

He wrote his testimony.

The aim of this work was outlined in its final paragraph, thus :-

"I pray God this little sketch may animate those who shall peruse it to praise the exceeding riches of His good-ness to an unworthy wretch."

Having made a number of copies of these letters, John Newton distributed them to interested friends, in the autumn of 1762.

One of these friends was Thomas Haweis, a clergyman from Christ Church, Oxford. There was something about Newton's story, and his style of writing, that immediately captured the imagination of his young acquaintance.

Haweis contacted John Newton with a request and a question. The request was for a more detailed account of the life story. An expansion of the letters. And the question was, "Would you still be prepared to consider ordination should an opportunity arise?"

The demand for an elaboration of the original eight letters pleased Newton. He set to work at once, re-writing and expanding the first account of his life, so that the eight letters became fourteen chapters of what he entitled, 'An Authentic Narrative'.

When completed, early in 1764, this work was sent to Thomas Haweis.

Perhaps discouraged by repeated rebuffs, the reply to the question about ordination, sent along with 'An Authentic Narrative', was rather brief and to the point. "My desire to serve the Lord is not weakened ; but I am not so hasty to push myself forward as I was formerly", he wrote.

A fortnight after receiving his copy of John Newton's life-story, Haweis contacted the author again. This time it was to inform John that Lord Dartmouth, an infuential peer who was also a Christian, had read 'An Authentic Narrative', and had been extremely impressed by it. He wanted a copy for himself.

After Newton had arranged for this personal copy to be forwarded, the Earl was so fascinated that he set up a meeting with its author.

Lord Dartmouth instantly recognised in this intense, and obviously well-read man, a depth of knowledge and experience that could be greatly used by God. So he determined to assist him by every possible means.

This help came in two ways. Firstly, he introduced John Newton to some of the most prominent and powerful men in England at that time. One of these was John Thornton, reputed to be the richest merchant in the country, and set to be a tremendous benefactor to the work which John Newton was soon about to embark upon for God.

Perhaps more significantly at the time, however, was the fact that Lord Dartmouth offered to John Newton the curacy of the parish church of St. Peter and St. Paul in the little town of Olney, in Buckinghamshire.

Newton accepted. Here was the opportunity that he had been waiting for. God had opened up the way for his diligent servant, at last. Just one slight snag, though. He still wasn't ordained into the ministry of the church. How would the dallying, demurring Bishops react when he reapplied for ordination?

His initial application was to the Archbishop of London, who received the would-be minister graciously, but started to make all sorts of excuses why he couldn't ordain a middle-aged evangelically-enthusiastic Methodist-loving ex-mariner. Unwilling to offend the quietly potent Lord Dartmouth, the Archbishop suggested that he had no doubt that the Bishop of Lincoln would ordain him.

So, armed with a letter of introduction from William Legge, second Earl of Dartmouth, John Newton set out to seek ordination, yet again. This time, though, things were different. After discussing church affairs and personal beliefs with the applicant for more than an hour, the Bishop of Lincoln declared himself, "satisfied". On 29th April, 1764, John Newton became a Clerk in Holy Orders of the Church of England.

The long wait was over. He had waited patiently for that moment. For almost six years.

On his way back to Liverpool to settle up his affairs, he made a short detour.

He just couldn't resist the temptation to spend an hour or two in Olney. "Just to take a glance at the place and the people."

As he dismounted below the towering elms, in Olney's market square, did he remember the words he had written to Mary in a letter, a few days earlier?

"I trust if the Lord sends me to Olney He will enable me to preach the glad tidings of Salvation."

The Lord who had saved him had, "appointed him to sanctuary service".

And the Lord who had, "appointed him to sanctuary service", had led him to Olney.

Surely He could help him "to preach the glad tidings of Salvation", as well.

6

Depressed And Dejected

---------------------- ❖ ----------------------

IN 1763, WHEN JOHN NEWTON WAS SEEKING GOD'S
GUIDANCE IN HIS LIFE, AND PUTTING THE FINAL
TOUCHES TO HIS EXPANDED 'AUTHENTIC NARRA-
TIVE', A TOTALLY DIFFERENT DRAMA WAS UNFOLD-
ING IN THE CITY OF LONDON.

It concerned a thirty-two year old barrister called William
Cowper.

This young man was well connected. He came from an
aristocratic family. His cousin, Major Cowper, was Clerk of
Parliaments and thus responsible for the entire staff of the
House of Lords. His influential kinsman had offered the
brilliant William, who appeared to be more interested in reading literature and writing poetry than working at anything, a
post in the upper House. As Clerk of the Journals.

The prospect of this position, and the apparent ease of its
acquisition, appealed to the basically-shy William Cowper.

As with many things in that bashful barrister's life, not everything was set to run smoothly, however. Some members of the Lords insisted that the prospective new Clerk of the Journals present himself for cross-examination at the Bar of the House so that his suitability for the position could be properly determined.

Contemplation of such an interview posed problems for William. Big, big problems.

This examination would require specialist knowledge of the purpose and functions of the Journals of the House of Lords. Knowledge which William didn't have and which he was was merely half-hearted in setting about to obtain. Even when he did drag himself to a study of the Journals, he found that the staff of the Records office, who didn't seem to like the "jobs-for-the-boys" employment policy which was so prevalent in those days, were totally uncooperative. This was distressing.

But far more distressing to the reclusive academic was the thought of an oral examination before a number of learned gentlemen. He felt increasingly that he just couldn't face it. Writing his Memoir of those days, later, he described his struggle to come to terms with the Journals :-

> *"I read without perception, for almost half a year altogether. My feelings were those of a man when he arrives at the place of execution."*

This was yet another barrier in the obstacle race which was called the life of William Cowper, to date. The course hadn't been by any means a straight run through. It had been littered with obstacles. Each one difficult to cope with in its different way.

The first of these traumas was the death of his mother when he was just six years of age. Anne Donne, a descendant of John Donne, the metaphysical poet and Dean of St. Pauls, had married Dr. John Cowper. They had a number of children who died in infancy, and two surviving sons, William and John.

The devastating effect of his gentle and intelligent mother's death on the timid William can best be described in the words of a poignant poem he wrote some fifty years after the event. A cousin sent him a miniature painting, in oils, that she had discovered amongst family memorabilia. It was of his mother. William expressed his reaction, in the best way he knew how. In verse :-

"My mother! when I learn'd that thou wast dead,
Say, wast thou conscious of the tears I shed?
Hover'd thy spirit o'er thy sorrowing son,
Wretch even then, life's journey just begun?
Perhaps thou gavest me, though unfelt, a kiss;
Perhaps a tear, if souls can weep in bliss—
Ah, that maternal smile!—it answers—Yes.
I heard the bell toll'd on thy burial day,
I saw the hearse that bore thee slow away,
And, turning from my nursery window, drew
A long, long sigh, and wept a last adieu..."

(From, 'On The Receipt Of My Mother's Picture Out Of Norfolk.' 1790.)

After the death of his wife, Dr. Cowper sent son William off to boarding school, where life was an absolute misery. The shy, thoughtful, and at-lessons-successful child, was mercilessly bullied by a domineering fifteen year old, "strong in arm, and weak in head." In some of his later writings, Cowper tells of the terror he experienced:-

"I well remember being afraid to lift my eyes upon him
higher than his knees, and I knew him by his shoe buckles
better than by any other part of his dress."

When he was ten years old, William moved on in his education. He was sent to Westminster School. Here he was only slightly happier, for although he was very clever and excelled academically, especially in languages, he was also acutely sensitive and was still bullied both verbally and physically. It was at Westminster School also that he discovered the enjoyment of, "both cricket and foot-ball".

Upon leaving school at eighteen, William became an apprentice to the law, working in a London solicitor's office. His move out into the big wide world of work, caused the reticent but talented young Cowper to reflect upon his social development. Or the lack of it. Again he expressed his conclusions, somewhat humorously, in verse:-

> "William was once a bashful youth;
> His modesty was such,
> That one might say (to say the truth)
> He rather had too much.
>
> But some a different notion had,
> And at each other winking,
> Observed, that though he little said,
> He paid it off with thinking.
>
> Howe'er, it happened, by degrees,
> He mended and grew perter ;
> In company was more at ease,
> And dressed a little smarter;
>
> Nay, now and then would look quite gay,
> As other people do ;
> And sometimes said, or tried to say,
> A witty thing or two.

The women said, who thought him rough,
But now no longer foolish,
"The creature may do well enough,
But wants a deal of polish."...!

(From, 'Of Himself' 1754.)

Also, during the period of his apprenticeship, William fell in love with an attractive and vivacious young woman. The only problem was, though, that she was his cousin, Theadora Cowper. The pair of them enjoyed each others company and conversation very much. Indeed, the love-struck William wrote more than a dozen poems to, or about, Theadora. Delia, he called her in his verses.

Although this friendship helped William to develop his skill as a poet, it did nothing to improve his mental stability. For it ended in ultimate disappointment. William's uncle, and Theadora's father, Ashley Cowper, called a halt to it. Said it wasn't good for either of them. Whether he was unhappy with the consanguinity of the relationship, or whether he detected in his nephew any hint of his impending madness, or whether indeed he was worried by William's increasing preoccupation with his own sense of inadequacy before God, is a matter of conjecture. We will probably never know for sure.

What is certain, though, is that the relationship ceased, abruptly, in 1756.

The farewell to Theadora, plus the death of his father in the same year, and the tragic death in a drowning accident of a close friend, Sir William Russell, in 1757, led to William Cowper feeling very lonely. The sense of isolation he experienced is pathetically portrayed in a poem which he wrote at the time :-

"Doomed as I am, in solitude to waste
The present moments, and regret the past ;

Deprived of every joy I valued most,
My friend torn from me, and my mistress lost...
Still, still I mourn, with each returning day,
Him snatched by fate in early youth away ;
And her—through tedious years of doubt and pain,
Fixed in her choice, and faithful—but in vain."...

(From, 'Disappointment.' 1757.)

Having eventually qualified in law, Cowper entered the Inner Temple as a barrister. But he was no lawyer. He had other more absorbing literary interests, contributing to a number of publications both in prose and in verse.

In an attempt, perhaps, to dispel the "dejection of spirits" that often afflicted him, he joined the Nonsense Club, whose membership was restricted to former students of Westminster School. Many of the members had been William's contemporaries and they idled away numerous hours together discussing literature and politics. And "giggling and making giggle".

The superficial mirth of the Club yielded Cowper only a temporary diversion, however, for he gradually became ever more conscious of a want, a lack, an emptiness in his life. There was something missing. It was a void that neither poetic composition or polite conversation could fill.

All that.

And now this.

How could he ever face a cross-examination in the House of Lords on a subject that he had tried in vain both to acquire a specific interest in, or obtain sufficient information about?

There was only the one way out of this whole depressing mess, he concluded.

7

If At First You Don't Succeed ...

❖

SUICIDE. TAKING HIS OWN LIFE. THE FINAL EXIT.
If he didn't go mad before the examination date in November he would have to end it all. So terrified had the timorous Cowper become that he could see no other means of escape.

And he began to explore the possibilities. Moving amongst the taverns and chop-houses of the inner city, he discussed the ethics and options of taking his own life with a number of casual acquaintances. These people assured him that the ancient philosophers had regarded suicide as an honourable method of ridding oneself of the cares and problems of this world.

Obviously none of them had ever considered God. Or judgement. Or a life beyond.

As a first step towards putting his plan into action, William Cowper went into an apothecary's shop and ordered half-an-ounce of laudanum. It is small wonder, perhaps, that the customer sensed the apothecary observing him "narrowly". Despite whatever reservations he may have had, however, he sold Cowper the drug. Consigning his purchase to a deep pocket, the would-be-suicide hurried from the shop.

Now I am prepared, at least, he thought.

On the day before the examination was due to take place, William Cowper was having breakfast in Richard's Coffee House, in Fleet Street. He picked up a morning newspaper and began to read it. Feeling persecuted and introspective, he concluded that the columnist was writing about him. And him alone. Personally. Particularly.

The article he read was, he supposed, mocking his timidity. It was challenging him to go and end his miserable existence. There and then. Once and for all.

His mind snapped.

He determined to do it. Immediately. Why waste time?

Leaving the coffee-house, he took a cab to Tower Wharf with the intention of jumping into the Thames. He would die like his friend had done some years before. By drowning.

Arriving at Custom House Quay he found it impossible to put that plan into action. For there wasn't enough water to drown himself in. In fact, there was no water at all. Just a layer of sticky, oozing mud. And there on the quayside, sitting on a pile of boxes and gazing nonchalantly all around him, was a porter. " A message to prevent me," Cowper later conceded.

Frustrated, he drove back to his chambers at the Inner Temple. There he had another go. He attempted to take the laudanum. Tried to poison himself.

Putting the phial to his lips he froze with fear. His whole body seemed to seize up. His hands refused to allow him to pour any of the lethal potion into his mouth. His fingers became, "closely contracted and entirely useless". And his throat seemed to seal up, too. He discovered that he couldn't swallow.

After repeated futile attempts, each one more frantic than the one before, Cowper realized that the ultimate option wasn't going to be achieved by poisoning either. He just couldn't do it. Some unseen power was holding him back.

Disgusted, he poured the poison into a bucket of dirty water that had been left sitting there, and tossed the empty phial out of the window.

Foiled again.

Next morning, when he heard the clock strike seven, William Cowper rose in a blind panic. The day appointed for his cross-examination in the House of Lords had arrived at last. And he was still alive! Just a few hours away from the dreaded interview!

Something had to be done! And fast!

He hadn't been able to drown himself.

He hadn't been able to poison himself.

There was yet another alternative he had often contemplated.

He could hang himself.

Tying one of his garters around his neck he climbed onto a chair and fastened the end of the garter to the top of the doorframe. Then he jumped off the chair.

This time it nearly worked.

He dangled for a few moments, and lost consciousness...

Then the garter broke.

When Cowper came round, he was lying face downwards on the floor. His neck had an ugly crimson ring around it, his eyes were bloodshot and swollen, and the side of his face was badly bruised from the fall.

Just as he was attempting to struggle to his feet, a maid blustered into the room.

She had heard the thump of him hitting the floor. Then silence. With her suspicions aroused she had come to investigate. Nothing had prepared her for the pathetic sight that met her gaze. She was totally shocked at the condition of her master.

William told her what he had just done. And asked her to summon help.

The frightened girl didn't need a second telling! Dashing from the room, and then from the house, she discovered Sir William Cowper having breakfast in a nearby coffee-house. Before collecting his cousin to escort him to the House of Lords. Or so he thought!

On accompanying the breathless maid back to William's room, the kind gentleman was appalled to observe the sorry state of the young lawyer. On hearing his explanation for this irrational and suicidal behaviour, Sir William exclaimed, "My dear Mr. Cowper, you terrify me! To be sure you can't hold the office (Clerk of the Journals) at this rate!..."

William Cowper, that morning, gave to his trying-so-hard-to-be-helpful cousin the keys to his drawer in the House of Lords, thus ending, in his own words, "all my connections with the Parliament House".

The plight of the poet was now serious.

He had lost his job. He was out of work.

He had lost his sanity. He was out of his mind.

But at least, he hadn't lost his life. He wasn't yet out of the reach of God's love and mercy.

And where there was life, and God, there was still hope.

8

"Do You Think I'm Mad?!"

❖

COWPER HAD LONGED FOR AN ESCAPE HATCH
THROUGH WHICH HE COULD CRAWL, AND THUS BE
RELIEVED OF THE PRESSURES AND CARES OF THIS
LIFE. AND TO A CERTAIN DEGREE HE HAD BEEN
GRANTED THAT RELIEF.

For he was now freed from the constraints of going to work.

He was not, though, nor could he be, it seemed, free from
an ever-increasing conviction of his own sinful nature. Walking backwards and forwards in his room, day after miserable
day, he decided that "there never was so abandoned a wretch,
so great a sinner", as himself. (And at that time he may not
have read Paul's self-assessment in 1 Timothy 1v15, and he
certainly had never met John Newton.)

William Cowper was convinced that a God of wrath and
vengeance was watching his every move and recording his
every thought. Just ready to pounce in judgement when He
had amassed sufficient evidence.

Putting the thoughts of those days into verse in a poem entitled, 'Hatred and Vengeance', he reckoned himself to be, "Damned below Judas ; more abhorred than he was," and "Buried above ground".

It seemed to be all doom and gloom.

His brother John, on hearing of his illness, came to visit him. And on seeing the state of him, stayed.

They talked. Discussed. Day and night.

John was a decent, religious man, but not as yet a Christian. So he only partially understood the spiritual anguish of his brother. During one conversation William suddenly stopped mid-sentence and lamented to John, "Oh, brother I am damned. Damned. Think of eternity, and think of what it is to be damned!"

When John, and other observers, noted that the matters perplexing William were "mainly of the religious kind" they sent for yet another of his cousins, Rev. Martin Madan, to come and visit him. Rev. Madan was an evangelical clergyman in the Church of England. If anybody could afford solace to a soul in turmoil, perhaps he could, they supposed. At the very least, perhaps he could talk some sense into the by-now apparently-hopelessly deranged Cowper.

Martin Madan responded to the invitation to visit his ailing cousin, and when he did, he recognised William's basic need straightaway, despite his unstable mental condition. He was seeking salvation.

The forthright minister was an imposing character. Well-mannered but not weak. Strong in will but gracious in spirit. And an ardent preacher of the Gospel.

Opening the Scriptures with William Cowper on a number of occasions, he was able to direct the anxious soul to three truths that he had never realized before.

The first was that all men are guilty before God. When he spoke of "original sin, and the corruption of every man born into the world, whereby every one is a child of wrath," Cowper actually felt somewhat relieved. At least he wasn't, as he had up until that moment believed, the only one condemned to be punished for his sin.

Then Madan explained how that Christ had died on the cross to atone for all the sins of the world. Including his. Cousin William confessed later that his "heart began to burn" when he came to appreciate the real meaning of the Saviour's death on Calvary.

The final bit was the most difficult one for Cowper. The sincere minister urged him to accept Jesus Christ as his Saviour. To come to a living faith in Him. "Not an assent only of the understanding, but a faith of application, an actually laying hold of it, and embracing it as a salvation wrought out," by God for him, personally.

This was too much for the poet. Much too much.

How he only wished that he could believe.

But he just couldn't. Not yet, anyway.

And things grew worse.

Both his mental and physical state deteriorated rapidly.

Soon he was afflicted with terrible blinding headaches. His speech became slurred. Then totally incoherent at times.

Something would have to be done.

John Cowper, Martin Madan, and Madan's assistant. Rev. Thomas Haweis, consulted on the matter. And it didn't take them long to reach a conclusion.

Brother John and cousin Martin went to inform William of their decision. They were sending him to be cared for in Dr.Cotton's asylum in St. Albans.

On hearing this William Cowper became verbally abusive. And very obstinate. An asylum! He was definitely not going into any asylum!

As a teenager he had paid a small fee to stand for hours with other sightseers and laugh at the antics of the inmates of Bedlam, the London asylum.

And now his friends were suggesting consigning him to just such a place!

No way!

"DO YOU THINK I'M MAD?!" he yelled.

9

The Sun Of Righteousness

❖

KEEPING COOL, JOHN COWPER ENGAGED IN SOME GENTLE PERSUASION.

When his older brother became sufficiently controlled to ask, "Do you really think it will do me good?", he knew that the rebellion was almost over.

"Yes. I believe it will", John replied emphatically.

William relented. Agreed to go.

So, in December 1763, William Cowper travelled to St. Albans, accompanied by John, and was admitted as a patient to Dr. Cotton's "Collegium Insanorum".

Nathaniel Cotton was a highly-respected doctor of medicine. But he was more than that . He was also a fairly successful poet, giving him a kindred interest with his newest patient. Most important of all, though, was the fact that he was a zealous Christian. A vital aspect of his treatment programme for the mentally-ill under his care was a discussion of spiritual matters, as the occasion arose. He considered it critical to address not only the needs of the body and mind, but also the need of the soul. Most rooms contained a copy of the Bible.

For the first six months of his stay at St. Albans, William continued "in bondage". Although he showed some interest in Dr. Cotton's stories, and by way of reply told a story or two of his own, a "conviction of sin, and expectation of judgement", never left him.

In the summer of 1764, John Cowper visited his brother, and although disappointed that William hadn't as yet made a complete recovery, he was encouraged that he had progressed sufficiently to be allowed to walk alone out in the garden.

After having a meal together, William began to feel some of the burden of gloom lift from his soul. Describing the experience later, he recalled :-

> *"Something like a ray of hope was shot into my heart ; but still I was afraid to indulge it. I spent the afternoon in a more cheerful manner. Something seemed to whisper to me, "Still there is mercy.""*

This revelation, that he was not yet beyond the mercy of God, greatly encouraged Cowper. Through conversation with Dr. Cotton, and his own personal reading, he searched for further enlightenment. And it came. Like this :-

> *"Having found a Bible on the bench in the garden, I opened upon the 11th of St. John, where Lazarus is raised from the dead ; and saw so much benevolence, mercy, goodness, and sympathy with miserable men, in our Saviour's conduct, that I almost shed tears upon the relation; little thinking that it was an exact type of the mercy which Jesus was on the point of extending towards*

myself. I sighed, and said, "Oh, that I had not rejected so good a Redeemer, that I had not forfeited all his favours." Thus was my heart softened, but not yet enlightened..."

The reading of that passage obviously led the searching soul, and beleagured mind, of the poet, to realize that God still loved him. Even him. With all his sense of guilt and imperfection. With all his fear of coming, and merited, judgement. There was still mercy. And forgiveness. And hope.

In late July, William Cowper had a marvellous, life-transforming, spiritual experience.

He was sitting in a chair near the window after breakfast, and had again picked up one of the ever-available Bibles. Still searching for the ultimate relief. Peace in his mind and calm in his soul.

The first verse he read was Romans 3 v. 25, and the truth of the words dawned upon him. Like further rays of light penetrating into the deepest and darkest recesses of his innermost being. Illuminating everything.

He read it again.

The verse, referring to Christ Jesus, stated :-

"Whom God hath set forth to be a propitiation through faith in his blood, to declare his righteousness for the remission of sins that are past, through the forbearance of God ;"

That was it ! What he had been looking for ! For all these years !

"A propitiation through faith in his blood..."

"Remission for sins that are past..."

The depth and reality of the moment of Cowper's conversion can best be described in his own words, written shortly afterwards :-

*"Immediately I received the strength to believe it, and the
full beams of the Sun of Righteousness shone upon me.
I saw the sufficiency of the atonement He had made, my
pardon sealed in His blood, and all the fulness and
completeness of His justification. In a moment I believed
and received the gospel. Whatever my friend Madan had
said to me, long before, recurred to me with the clearest
evidence of its truth, "with demonstration of the Spirit
and with power." Unless the Almighty Arm had been
under me, I think I should have died with gratitude and
joy. My eyes filled with tears, and my voice choked with
transport ; I could only look up to Heaven in silence,
overwhelmed with love and wonder!"*

William Cowper was saved! And changed !

All the sense of guilt and fear of judgement had disappeared.

The peace of God, which passes all understanding, had taken over his heart and mind, through Christ Jesus. It was, indeed, almost unbelievable.

And Dr. Cotton, sincere Christian that he was, and praying for just such a breakthrough as he doubtless had been, when it came to the bit was rather cautious. Gave his patient time to prove the reality of his experience. But he needn't have worried. When he observed, day by day, the tranquility of mind and lightness of spirit that the poet seemed to enjoy, he was thoroughly convinced. William had told him one day that he was so happy that he didn't want to go to bed and waste time asleep!

It was not surprising, then, that Cowper expressed his profound happiness and contentment in verse. During the months following his conversion he penned a number of poems, describing his early anguish of soul and pouring out his heart in thanksgiving to the Saviour, for the peace and joy which he had found.

In one of them he describes his progression from the "fiery deeps of sharp conviction" to witnessing to the wonders of "grace divine". Six of the original thirteen stanzas allow us to identify the spiritual landmarks in his experience with God :-

A Song of Mercy and Judgement.

Lord, I love the habitation
Where the Saviour's honour dwells;
At the sound of thy salvation
With delight my bosom swells.
Grace divine, how sweet the sound,
Sweet the grace which I have found.

Me through waves of deep affliction,
Dearest Saviour! thou hast brought,
Fiery deeps of sharp conviction
Hard to bear and passing thought.
Sweet the sound of grace divine,
Sweet the grace which makes me thine.

But at length a word of healing
Sweeter than an angel's note,
From the Saviour's lips distilling
Chased despair and changed my lot.
Sweet the sound of grace divine,
Sweet the grace which made me thine.

"I", He said, "have seen thee grieving,
Loved thee as I passed thee by;
Be not faithless, but believing,
Look, and live, and never die."
Sweet the sound of grace divine,
Sweet the grace which makes me thine.

All at once my chains were broken,
From my feet my fetters fell,
And that word in pity spoken,
Snatched me from the gates of hell.
Grace divine , how sweet the sound,
Sweet the grace which I have found.

Since that hour, in hope of glory,
With thy followers I am found,
And relate the wondrous story
To thy listening saints around.
Sweet the sound of grace divine
Sweet the grace which makes me thine.

Another is one of the very first hymns he ever wrote. Cowper himself described it later as, "a specimen of my first Christian thoughts, being written shortly after my conversion." In it the sweet release of his salvation is evident. The Sun of Righteousness had transformed the "dreary province" of his soul.

Behold I Make All Things New.

How blest Thy creature is, O God,
When with a single eye,
He views the lustre of Thy Word,
The day-spring from on high.

Thro' all the storms that veil the skies
And frown on earthly things;
The Sun of Righteousness he eyes
With healing in His wings.

Struck by that light, the human heart,
A barren soil no more,
Sends the sweet smell of Grace abroad,
Where serpents lurked before.

The soul, a dreary province once,
Of Satan's dark domain;
Feels a new empire formed within,
And owns a heavenly reign.

The glorious orb, whose silver beams,
The fruitful year control
Since first, obedient to Thy word,
He started from the goal;

Has cheer'd the nations, with the joys
His orient rays impart,
But JESUS, 'tis Thy light alone,
Can shine upon the heart.

(Olney Hymns. Book 3. Hymn 44.)

The now calm-and-content Cowper was in no hurry to leave St. Albans. He felt serene and secure there. Every morning he enjoyed "sweet communion with Dr. Cotton on the things concerning our salvation."

Much as he would have loved to, William Cowper couldn't stay in the cosy atmosphere of Dr. Cotton's College for the remainder of his life, however.

He was going to have to move out. Move on. Move away. But to where?

Where could a newly-born-again, but out-of-work, thirty-four-year-old poet, go to, on his release from a mental institution?

His brother John made a series of tentative enquiries on his behalf. And drew a series of blanks.

Becoming more acutely aware of his need of somewhere to live in the world outside, and also of an increasing enjoyment of, and craving for, the warmth of Christian fellowship, Cowper brought the matter to God in prayer. Telling of his concern and his earnest request, he says :-

> *"I one day poured out my heart in prayer before the Lord, beseeching Him that wherever He should be pleased in His fatherly mercy to lead me, it might be into the society of those that feared His name and loved the Lord Jesus in sincerity..."*

But God had already His plan in place for William Cowper. He didn't know that yet, though.

10

A Richer Blessing

❖

EARLY ONE JUNE MORNING IN 1765, WILLIAM
COWPER MADE THE BIG BREAK. DARED TO VENTURE
OUT AGAIN INTO THE WORLD AT LARGE. HE LEFT
ST. ALBANS.

After a solemn farewell with Dr. Cotton, he travelled to a
rented room which brother John had procured for him in
Huntingdon, Cambridgeshire.

For a while he enjoyed the freedom. The liberty. The calm
of mind and soul. And the bustle of everyday life, rippling on
all around him. But gradually he began to feel lonely. Felt a
growing yearning for the warmth of Christian fellowship.
Missed his daily discussions with Dr.Cotton.

On a Saturday evening he set off for a walk in the country.
Just to pass the time. And be alone with his thoughts. He felt
a bit downhearted. Almost melancholy.

Suddenly he felt a strong desire to pray. To speak to God about it.

He describes what happened :-

> *"Having gained a retired and secret nook in the corner of a field, I knelt under a bank and poured out my complaints before Him. It pleased my Saviour to hear me, so that the oppression under which I had laboured was entirely taken off. I was enabled to trust in Him..."*

The next morning he went to church for the first time since his conversion. He found himself able to worship God with a new insight and vigour. "Beheld the fair beauty and glory of the Lord", as never before.

Cowper, who for a few weeks had "felt like a traveller in the midst of an inhospitable desert, without a friend to comfort or guide him", was greatly encouraged by that service. Having heard the Word of God read and expounded with genuine sincerity, and having experienced anew the closeness of Christian communion, he:-

> *"went immediately after church to the place where I had prayed the day before and found that the relief I had then received was but the earnest of a richer blessing."*

That "richer blessing" was to come in the form of a life-long friendship with a family. And in particular, a person.

Unknown to him, the members of a certain family had become curious about the distinguished-looking stranger who had started to attend their church every Sunday. He had an air of respectable sophistication about him that fascinated them.How they would love to meet him! Find out who he was!

Eventually, one Sunday morning, the son of the family, William Unwin, invited the lone visitor round to their house for afternoon tea that day.

William Cowper was delighted to accept the invitation. And the resulting invitation to join them for lunch on the next Sunday!

Such sweet communion did they enjoy on those first two Sunday visits that Cowper became a very regular and much appreciated caller at the Unwin's red-brick house in Huntingdon High Street.

There were four of them in the family.

Rev. Morley Unwin was a local parish minister, and his wife Mary was an intelligent, well-read, dedicated Christian. They had two children, William, who was twenty-one when he was given the pleasant task of approaching the poet, and his young sister Susanna, who was eighteen.

William Cowper was welcomed by this family as one of the family. They enjoyed his company. And his conversation. The shy gentleman with the fluent flow of language had so much to tell. And so eloquently. About life. About London. About love for his Lord...

He, in turn, rejoiced in their willingness to listen to, and share with, him. He relished the genuine nature of their friendship. And "gave thanks to God who had so graciously answered the prayer", which he had, "preferred to Him at St.Albans." By bringing him into, "the society of Christians". So friendly did they all become that on 11th November, 1765, William Cowper moved into the Unwin home as a paying guest. For him this was absolute bliss.

For more than a year everything went well. His life-style was most agreeable. Very pleasant, to say the least. He read extensively, wrote when he felt inspired, took long walks in the surrounding countryside, developed a kitchen garden and played battledore and shuttlecock with the family on fine days.

Spiritual matters were not forgotten, either. Top priority in the household was given to the things of God. They read, as a group, and collectively discussed, the Bible and a number of books on Christian topics. Two of their favourites were, 'The Rise and Progress of Religion in the Soul', by Philip Doddridge, and 'An Authentic Narrative', which told in graphic detail the wonderful experiences of its author, one John Newton. How they all, but particularly William Cowper and Mary Unwin, often expressed a desire to meet this, "Mr. Newton"!

In addition to their reading, and "much religious conversation", they also enjoyed singing the hymns from Rev. Martin Madan's new collection, compiled chiefly from the work of Isaac Watts and Charles Wesley, and entitled simply, 'Psalms and Hymns'. Mrs. Unwin accompanied the singing on the harpsichord, and Cowper remarked once, upon reflection on those, "tolerable concerts", that, "our hearts were by far the best and most musical performers"!

Describing those idyllic days at Huntingdon, with the Unwins, in a letter to his aunt in October, 1766, Cowper writes :-

> *"I need not tell you that such a life as this is consistent with the utmost cheerfulness. Accordingly, we are all happy, and dwell together in unity, as brethren. Mrs. Unwin has almost a maternal affection for me, and I have something like a filial one for her, and her son and I are brothers. Blessed be the God of my Salvation for such companions..."*

Almost too good to last?
It was.

11

Instant Bonding

❖

IN LATE JUNE, 1767, TRAGEDY STRUCK. UPSET THE
COSY LITTLE SET-UP.

Rev. Morley Unwin was riding to conduct a Sunday
service, in a church some miles from his home in Huntingdon,
when he was thrown from his horse. He sustained a fractured
skull and died from his injuries four days later.

In the midst of her grief, Mary Unwin had a pressing
problem to address. The house in which they were living
belonged to the church, and would be required, in the process
of time, for Morley's successor. So she had to find a new home
for the family. And for the lodger, who by that time was looked
upon as part of the family.

She prayed for guidance as to where they should move.
Mrs. Unwin had only one specific request that she desired of
God. That that He would lead them to a place where they
could "sit under" an evangelical minister.

Just as He had done for William Cowper, almost two years before, God was prepared to answer her prayers also. His Development Plan for the Unwin family, plus paying guest, was already in place.

A few days after Rev. Unwin's death a friend of both families informed Rev. John Newton of Mrs. Unwin's tragic bereavement.

Rev. Newton, touched by the heart-breaking nature of the event, and ever ready to minister to the needs of sick and sorrowing Christians, rode over to Huntingdon to tender his condolences to the widow. Bring her solace from the Word of God.

When they met, Mary Unwin immediately warmed to the frank ex-seaman. Straight and true he was, yet unbelievably gentle with it. And Newton liked her too. Saw in her a genuine, thoughtful believer.

Perhaps the more important meeting that took place in that house of mourning, however, was the first encounter between John Newton, converted sea captain, now curate at Olney, and William Cowper, converted poet and intellectual, now lodger at Unwins.

The two men were at one at once. They felt a total affinity with each other from that first moment of meeting.

William Cowper was thrilled to meet the author of , 'An Authentic Narrative'.

John Newton was thrilled to meet a wizard-with-words like William Cowper.

But there was even more to it than that.

Although they looked so different physically, for Newton was weather-beaten and tough whereas Cowper was pale and refined, they were so alike in so many ways.

Each had lost his mother in early childhood

Each had endured unsettling experiences in his teenage years.

Each had successfully expressed his thoughts in poetry.

Each had been close to death on more than one occasion.

But each had come to a point in his life when he had undergone a genuine life-changing experience with God.

Each of them had been saved.

At different times. In different places. Under different circumstances.

And it was the fact that they were both children of God that forged the vital link. That bonded them together instantly.

They had lots in common.

On discovering that the Unwin extended-family were contemplating moving away from Huntingdon, John Newton at once suggested that they come to Olney. He even offered to make enquiries with a view to securing somewhere for them to live in the town, so pleased was he at the prospect of their company.

Mary Unwin and her paying guest immediately greeted this proposal with real enthusiasm. They were thrilled at the thought! Imagine! Living in the same town as, and savouring the ministry of, the Rev. Newton, day after day, week after week! What could be better?!

God had guided again. Answered their prayers once more.

So, on 14th September, 1767, Mary and Susanna Unwin and William Cowper, their house guest, moved to Olney. William Unwin was studying at Cambridge, and thus did not need to come with them.

Whilst looking for somewhere permanent of their own to live, the three new residents of the little Buckinghamshire town stayed with John and Mary Newton, who were themselves in temporary accommodation since the vicarage was being refurbished. The cramped conditions didn't seem to mar in any way the fellowship that they all enjoyed with each other from that very first early autumn day.

A wonderful rapport began to develop amongst them all, almost at once.

And that was only the start!

12

A Closer Walk With God

❖

THE THRILL OF THOSE EARLY DAYS OF FELLOWSHIP
IN OLNEY COULDN'T REALLY BE EXPECTED TO LAST
FOREVER. LIFE DOESN'T USUALLY WORK OUT LIKE
THAT. AND IT DIDN'T.

Something had to happen to bring them all down to earth
with a bump. And it did.

Mary Unwin took ill. Very ill. So ill that everyone was
convinced that she was going to die. Having lived through
two of the most traumatic experiences a human being can
endure, the death of her husband and moving house,
Mrs. Unwin's health deteriorated rapidly in late October.

This illness greatly distressed William Cowper, who
thought that he was about to lose the one person on earth
who had shown him most care and kindness. His genuine
concern is manifested in a letter which he wrote to his aunt,
Mrs. Madan, in early December. Not only does this letter

indicate something of the poet's affection for Mary Unwin, but it also demonstrates two other things. It allows us to ascertain something of the deepening nature of Cowper's spiritual experience, with his emphasis on the importance of prayer and his desire to do the will of God in his life. We are also given an insight into the circumstances surrounding the writing of one of his earliest hymns, which is still being sung today. It shows something of the blend of poetic flair and Divine inspiration that are required to produce an effective and lasting hymn. Thus the letter is best quoted in full.

> *Dear Aunt,*
>
> *I should not have suffered your last kind Letter to have laid by me so long   unanswer'd, had it not been for many Hindrances and especially One, which h a s e n g a g e d much of my Attention. My dear Friend Mrs. Unwin, whom the Lord gave me to be a Comfort to me in that Wilderness from which he has just delivered me, has been for many Weeks in so declining a way, and has suffered so many Attacks of the most excruciating Pain, that I have hardly been able to keep alive the faintest Hope of her Recovery. I know that our God heareth Prayer, and I know that he hath opened mine and many Hearts amongst this People to pray for her. Here lies my chief Support, without which I should look upon myself as already deprived of her. Again when I consider the great Meetness to which the Lord has wrought her for the Inheritance in Light, her most exemplary Patience under the sharpest Sufferings, her truly Christian Humility and Resignation, I am more than ever inclined to believe that her Hour is come. Let me engage your Prayers for Her, and for Me. You know what I have most need of upon an Occasion like this: Pray that I may receive it at His Hands*

from whom every good and perfect Gift proceeds. She is the chief Blessing I have met with in my Journey since the Lord was pleased to call me, and I hope the Influence of her edifying and Excellent Example will never leave me. Her Illness has been a sharp Trial to me—Oh that it may have a sanctified Effect, that I may rejoice to Surrender up to the Lord my dearest Comforts the Moment he shall require them. Oh! for no Will but the Will of my Heavenly Father! Dr. Cotton for whose advice we went together to St.Albans about a Month since, seemed to have so little Expectation that Medicine could help her, that he might be said to give her over. He prescribed however, but she has hardly been able to take his Medicines. Her Disorder is a Nervous Atrophy   attended with violent Spasms of the Chest and Throat, and This is a bad Day with her; worse than common.

I return you many Thanks for the Verses you favor'd me with, which speak sweetly the Language of the Christian Soul. I wish I could pay you in kind, but must be contented to pay you in the best kind I can. I began to compose them Yesterday Morning before Daybreak, but fell asleep at the End of the two first Lines, when I awaked again the third and fourth were whispered to my Heart in a way which I have often experienced.

Oh for a closer Walk with God,
 A calm & heav'nly Frame,
 A light to shine upon the Road
 That leads me to the Lamb !

Where is the Blessedness I knew
 When first I saw the Lord?
 Where is the Soul-refreshing View
 Of Jesus in his Word?

What peacefull Hours I then enjoy'd,
  How sweet their Mem'ry still!
But they have left an Aching Void
  The World can never fill.

Return, O Holy Dove, Return,
  Sweet Messenger of Rest,
I hate the Sins that made thee mourn
  And drove thee from my Breast.

The dearest Idol I have known,
  Whate'er that Idol be,
Help me to tear it from Thy Throne,
  And worship Only Thee.

Then shall my Walk be close with God,
  Calm and serene my Frame,
Then purer Light shall mark the Road
  That leads me to the Lamb.

*Yours my dear Aunt in the Bands of that Love which
cannot be quenched.*

Wm. Cowper.
Olney. Dece. 10. 67.

(Walking with God. Genesis 5v.24.
Olney Hymns. Book 1. Hymn 3)

13

The Guinea Field

❖

THANKFULLY, GOD ANSWERED THE MANY FERVENT PRAYERS OF MANY FERVENT CHRISTIANS, AGAIN. MRS UNWIN RECOVERED. SHE WAS GRADUALLY, BUT WONDERFULLY, RESTORED TO HEALTH. COWPER'S 'DEAREST IDOL' WAS NOT TO BE REMOVED FROM HIM. IN THE MEANTIME, AT LEAST.

On 15th February 1768, William Cowper and Mary and Susanna Unwin moved into the new residence which John Newton had helped them to procure, called Orchard Side. In one of his first letters to Mrs. Madan, after they had moved in, Cowper referred to it as 'our own mansion'. That, perhaps, was a rather flattering description, but it was a big house. So big, indeed, that half of it, the half beside the poorer cottages, had been shut off, boarded up. Nobody, it was reckoned, would need the rambling, falling-down side of the building. The rats lived in that bit.

Orchard Side was, and still is, situated on the Market Square in Olney. Although having a large, almost barrack-like appearance from the outside,(William Unwin said it was 'more like a prison than a house'), the rooms inside were small. The living accommodation was cramped. And there were no 'mod-cons'. When the refined Mary Unwin saw the kitchen and the cooking 'facilities' it must surely have been enough to make her ill again. Bring on a relapse. They were primitive in the extreme!

One aspect of the location of Orchard Side pleased William Cowper. Another frequently annoyed him.

He was glad to have an unrestricted view out on to the Market Square. Just by sitting discreetly behind the curtains of the downstairs parlour he could observe the constant comings-and-goings of everyday life. Be a people watcher. In the market-place, beneath its three towering elms, stood the Town Hall which was a two-storied stone building, and a small hexagonal building. 'The Round House'. The prison. So there were always lots of people about. And no end of activity to watch, and contemplate. The alert mind of the poet revelled in that.

The down-side of Orchard Side, however, was that it was close to the River Ouse, and often pestilent mists crept up from the river, enveloping their end of town.

That mist was, in fact there to welcome the new tenants when they stepped out into the street on their first morning of permanent residence in their Olney home. The all-pervading, everything-dampening mist, perfumed by the stench of rotting vegetables abandoned after a previous market, hailed their arrival in Market Square!

But they were happy to be there, for so many reasons!

William Cowper was to derive great pleasure from the garden at the back of the house. Summer and winter alike. In summer he perfected his skill as a gardener, encouraged, as it was so to turn out in succeeding years, by Mary Newton, who was herself a gardening enthusiast. And during the winter, when the 'roads' around the little Buckinghamshire town were reduced to mud-tracks, and the fields were more-or-less swamps, Cowper satisfied his 'locomotive faculty' by walking up and down the thirty-yard path threaded through the garden.

Considering his plants. Consulting his Power. Composing his poetry.

Separated from Orchard Side by the orchard from which the house derived its name, was the recently refurbished Vicarage in which Rev. John Newton and his wife Mary had taken up residence.

The vicarage was a much more spacious building than Orchard Side. Newton, delighted with his permanent home, described it as 'one of the best and most commodious houses in the country'. William Cowper's description of the same building, after he had become a frequent visitor to it, was slightly more reserved. He found it to be, 'a smart stone building, well-sashed. Much too good for the living.'

The windows of Newton's study, on the top floor, overlooked the church, a large building with an impressive spire, Olney mill, and the bridge over the River Ouse.

To personalise that room John painted two texts on the plaster of the wall, just above the fireplace. To him they were a mirror of his own life. They served as a daily reminder of God's amazing grace that had transformed a blaspheming mariner into an evangelical minister. He wrote :-

Since thou wast precious in my sight, thou hast been honourable.
(Isaiah 43 v. 4)

> *But thou shalt remember that thou wast a bondman in*
> *the land of Egypt, and the Lord thy God redeemed thee.*
> *(Deuteronomy 15 v. 15)*

As the relationship between the Newtons, William Cowper and the Unwins deepened, they began to spend even more of their waking hours in each others' company. It was night about, every night, in the vicarage or Orchard Side. But there was just one problem.

Not a personal one. Nor, indeed, a spiritual one. It was a practical one.

Although there was only an orchard dividing the backs of the two properties, they were all having to make a round-about journey by road and lane to visit each other

Resourceful Newton and his friend, thoughtful Cowper, soon came up with an answer to that one. They approached Mrs. Asprey, the owner of the orchard, with a proposition, to which she agreed. For a fee. They obtained her permission to make a path through her orchard, thus avoiding the circuitous route round by the road.

John Newton soon knocked a hole in the wall at the back of his house and a path was then marked out through the orchard. Mrs Asprey charged the friends-and-neighbours an annual fee of one guinea for the use of their personal right-of-way.

Hence the orchard became known to them all as, "The Guinea Field".

And it was often traversed!

14

'God Made The Country ...'

---❖---

**'WE CAN SHEW YOU A BEAUTIFULL COUNTRY, THO'
NOT MUCH CELEBRATED IN SONG, AND A FINE LONG
TOWN, PRETTY CLEAN IN SUMMERTIME AND FULL
OF POOR FOLKS.'**

So wrote William Cowper to his friend Joseph Hill, on
Saturday, 7th May 1768. The countryside around his new home
town had obviously impressed him with its beauty. And the
description of the elongated nature of the town of Olney
itself, with its summer charm and impoverished population
was spot-on.

As the spring of 1768 eased itself gently into summer, two
friends were often to be seen tramping the streets of that 'fine
long town', and the fields and lanes immediately surrrounding
it, together. One was a robust ex-seaman. The other a frail-
looking poet. And they talked, and talked and talked.

There was so much to talk about. And share. And discuss.

John Newton could have spent half-a-walk telling his friend about some more interesting incidents from his eventful early life. Bits he had left out of the 'Authentic Narrative'. Remembered too late. Entertaining embellishments. Further proof of God's marvellous dealings with him. They would also discuss the voyage of a young sea-captain called James Cook who was setting out that year to explore the possibilities of establishing a colony in a strange and distant southern land called Australia. The ex-sea-captain would outline in precise detail all the difficulties of such a long sea-journey, to his land-locked listener.

William Cowper, in turn, would, no doubt, have demonstrated to his less well-educated companion, his in-depth knowledge of the classics. And they could have spent ages considering the merits of one of either of their most recent verse creations.

Newton was later to write, of his friendship with the poet, that 'never a day passed but we spent at least twelve hours of it in each other's company, when we were awake and at home'. And the townspeople of Olney were witnesses to that fact. They became used to seeing the two men together more frequently.

The Buckinghamshire town was an important centre for the production of hand-made lace in the mid-eighteenth century, and as the two companions walked through the streets they would always have a cheery word for the cottage lacemakers, the 'poor folks',who would be clustered out around their doors on fine days, plying their trade.

As they walked through the streets the two men would have passed a number of public houses. There were fifty-six of them in all, in the town, supplied by the local maltsters and breweries. So, whilst the women of Olney were engaged in cottage lace-making, many of the men worked by day in the breweries and spent their evenings sampling the local ales.

Striding together through the streets of the town was, for Newton and Cowper, usually only a means to an end. They were almost invariably on their way to somewhere else. The country.

In his oft-quoted line from 'The Task. Bk.1', Cowper states that :-

'God made the country, and man made the town.'

Obviously the two mens' preference was for the country. For that was always their ultimate destination. To pound the lanes and tracks through the neighbouring countyside. Or to meander by the meandering Ouse.

Both of them had alert minds. And keen eyes. They were ardent observers of Nature, and the intricate and beautiful details of the natural world, as this short extract from Book 1 of 'The Task', Cowper's long poem in six 'books', demonstrates. He describes a wood, with the beauty in variety of its different trees, and the River Ouse beyond :-

'No tree in all the grove but has its charms,
Though each its hue peculiar ; paler some,
And of a wannish gray ; the willow such,
And poplar, that with silver lines his leaf,
And ash far stretching his umbrageous arm ;
Of deeper green the elm ; and deeper still,
Lord of the woods, the long-surviving oak.
Some glossy-leaved, and shining in the sun,
The maple, and the beech of oily nuts
Prolific, and the lime at dewy eve
Diffusing odours : nor unnoted pass

The sycamore, capricious in attire,
Now green, now tawny, and, ere autumn yet
Have changed the woods, in scarlet honours bright.
O'er these, but far beyond (a spacious map
Of hill and valley interposed between,)
The Ouse, dividing the well-water'd land,
Now glitters in the sun, and now retires,
As bashful, yet impatient to be seen.'

These walks together were more than just pleasant, carefree country strolls, however. There was an over-riding spiritual dimension to all their discussions, and observations. On balmy summer days, and in the blustery but colourful autumn ones that followed, the intense poet and his curate friend, enjoyed sweet spiritual fellowship, discussed spiritual matters for protracted periods, and anticipated spiritual growth in their town and district.

Acute observation of the simple majesty of the wealth of Nature in the countryside which they traversed together almost daily, led the two thoughtful Christians to an even deeper appreciation of their God. Through His creation.

Cowper, in 'The Task, Book 6', explains this delightfully, ending in a rapturous crescendo. Oh the joy, not only of walking, or of walking with his soul-mate Newton, but of walking with God! :-

'Nature is but a name for an effect
Whose cause is God. He feeds the secret fire
By which the mighty process is maintain'd,
Who sleeps not, is not weary ; in whose sight
Slow-circling ages are as transient days ;
Whose work is without labour; whose designs
No flaw deforms, no difficulty thwarts ;
And whose beneficence no charge exhausts.

...One spirit— His
Who wore the platted thorns with bleeding brow—
Rules universal nature. Not a flower
But shews some touch in freckle, streak, or stain,
Of His unrivall'd pencil. He inspires
Their balmy odours and imparts their hues,
And bathes their eyes with nectar, and includes,
In grains as countless as the seaside sands,
The forms with which He sprinkles all the earth.
Happy who walks with Him!'

In addition to walking in the country, for pleasure, the two inseparable comrades often travelled together to the outlying villages where curate Newton was responsible for the conduct of church meetings. Occasionally, both the Marys came along as well, but often just Mary Unwin, who was an accomplished singer and thus an undoubted asset! When both of the ladies were unavailable, though, Newton and Cowper were happy to set out themselves.

In these small and remote meetings, attended by simple but sincere country folk, Rev. Newton encouraged his naturally reticent, but spiritually effervescent, companion to contribute in some way to the conduct of the worship.

Their mutual scouring of the countryside is mentioned frequently by Newton in his pocket-book for 1768. One such entry reads :-

' *September 19. Breakfasted at Yardley, spoke from Matt.*
v. 6. At Denton, from Phil. iv. 4. Mr. Cowper went with
me, a pleasant walk both ways.'

As the friendship between the two men of like mind began to deepen significantly, so too the work of God in Olney appeared to be flourishing. There was a genuine interest amongst the townspeople in attending church to hear the new and tireless, caring but fearless, curate preach.

And he had taught them the importance of prayer. Both in private and in public.

So much so that a larger room or building would have to be secured for the mid-week prayer meeting. Up until then they had been meeting in the home of Molly Mole, the house that Newton referred to wittily as "The Mole Hill", but it had by now become far too small. They just couldn't accommodate all those who turned up to pray.

A promising sign.

15

The Great House

❖

PROMPT ACTION WAS REQUIRED.

Many of the people of Olney, recently turned to the Saviour, wanted to attend church. And the mid-week prayer meetings.

An extra gallery, called the "Newton Gallery", was added to the church to cater for the huge Sunday crowds. But the mid-week services were more of a problem. The houses in which these meetings were being held just couldn't cope with the numbers who came any more. And the church building wasn't the answer. It would be too big and cold for the warmth and informal fire of the Newton-led prayer meetings.

The resourceful curate of Olney was always on the look-out for an opportunity to preach the Gospel. Teach the Scriptures. Encourage prayer. Assist the local community. And he soon came up with an idea.

Between the church and the mill stood an empty mansion known as 'The Great House'. John Newton recognised its potential as a meeting place. It would afford the relaxed cordiality of a home, and yet would be spacious enough, hopefully, to accommodate all who would choose to attend. Ideal.

He approached Lord Dartmouth, the owner, and requested permission to use it. This approval was readily granted by the generous Dartmouth, who had already been impressed by the spiritual impact that Newton's activities were having on the town and district.

Following a period of redecoration, the Great Room in The Great House was ready for use. John Newton was delighted with it, as it could hold, "over one hundred and thirty people".

Throughout his lifetime Newton always had a great sense of occasion. Birthdays, anniversaries and special events of all sorts were celebrated, and the celebration was usually marked with a poem, or hymn.

And so, for the official opening of The Great House, on 17th April, 1769, he asked William Cowper to compose an appropriate hymn, undertaking also to write one himself.

Both these hymns, which were penned for that specific event, and are still in use today, are given below. This affords a unique opportuniy to compare and contrast the poetic prowess of the two friends, as they both address the same subject.

Although Cowper later became accepted as a national poet in his own right, secular literary critics have been less than complimentary in their evaluation of Newton's work. Statements like, "Cowper was a poet, Newton merely a versifier", are not uncommon.

In all fairness, however, it must be stated that although differences in style, and indeed, of approach, can occasionally be traced in the work of these two Christian contemporaries from Olney, one thing is not, and was never, in question. Their sincerity.

Both of these gifted men set out to use their talents with
two clearly-defined aims. The glory of God, and the advancement of His gospel.

And God blessed their work to the 'poor folks' of Olney.
As He has done to thousands since.

The two hymns:-

On Opening a Place for Social Prayer.
(J. Newton)

O Lord, our languid souls inspire,
  For here, we trust, thou art!
Send down a coal of heav'nly fire,
  To warm each waiting heart.

Dear Shepherd of thy people, hear,
  Thy presence now display ;
As thou hast giv'n a place for prayer,
  So give us hearts to pray.

Shew us some token of thy love,
  Our fainting hope to raise ;
And pour thy blessings from above ,
  That we may render praise.

Within these walls let holy peace,
  And love, and concord dwell ;
Here give the troubled conscience ease,
  The wounded spirit heal.

The feeling heart, the melting eye,
  The humble mind bestow ;
And shine upon us from on high,
  To make our graces grow!

May we in faith receive thy word,
 In faith present our prayers ;
And, in the presence of our Lord,
 Unburden all our cares.

And may the gospel's joyful sound
 Enforc'd by mighty grace,
Awaken many sinners round,
 To come and fill the place.

(Olney Hymns. Book 2. Hymn 43)

On Opening a Place for Social Prayer.
(W. Cowper)

Jesus, where'er thy people meet,
There they behold thy mercy-seat ;
Where'er they seek thee thou art found,
And ev'ry place is hallow'd ground.

For thou, within no walls confin'd,
Inhabitest the humble mind ;
Such ever bring thee, where they come,
And going, take thee to their home.

Dear Shepherd of thy chosen few!
Thy former mercies here renew ;
Here, to our waiting hearts, proclaim
The sweetness of thy saving name.

Here may we prove the pow'r of pray'r,
To strengthen faith, and sweeten care ;
To teach our faint desires to rise,
And bring all heav'n before our eyes.

Behold at thy commanding word,
We stretch the curtain and the cord (a) ;
Come thou, and fill this wider space,
And help us with a large encrease.

Lord, we are few, but thou art near ;
Nor short thine arm, nor deaf thine ear ;
Oh rend the heav'ns, come quickly down,
And make a thousand hearts thine own!

(Olney Hymns. Book 2.Hymn 44.)
(a) Isaiah 54. 2

Imagine hearing the plain-spoken curate and the soft-spoken poet reading their own compositions to the assembled company!

There was no sense of competion. Just a real sense of God.

No wonder the people loved it!

No wonder the place was packed!

16

"As Happy As A King!"

❖

IN SEPTEMBER OF THAT SAME YEAR,1769, WILLIAM
COWPER RECEIVED AN URGENT CALL TO GO TO
CAMBRIDGE. HIS BROTHER JOHN, WHO WAS THE
MINISTER OF A PARISH JUST OUTSIDE THE CITY, WAS
ILL. SERIOUSLY ILL, IT SEEMED.

On arrival at his brother's bedside, William discovered that
his brother was, indeed, gravely ill. He had a fever, which
had developed from a cold.

William was concerned for his brother. Both physically and
spiritually.

Since his own conversion, William could never understand
John's apparent total lack of interest in his personal salvation.
Although a minister, his views on spiritual matters differed
widely from those of his older brother. He saw no need for
the evangelical faith. On his occasional visits to Olney he
had attended family prayers in Orchard Side, but had not

participated, and had attended church to hear Rev. John Newton preach, but had not approved.

For years, although William had spoken to John about Christian matters, as opportunity presented itself, his brother had always listened to him patiently, and courteously, but had never replied. Or reacted in any way.

William found this frustrating. But John had his reasons for this behaviour.

So great was the chasm between his beliefs and those of his brother, who appeared to be totally obsessed with Christ and the gospel, that he had decided that this policy of non-response was the most effective method of avoiding embarrassing disagreements between them.

He tried not to seem even remotely interested in this 'gospel of the grace of God.' Anyway, it could seriously damage your peace of mind to spend time thinking about things like sin and salvation. Heaven and hell. Time and eternity.

As later events were to prove, however, William's witness, right from the time of his conversion in St. Albans, until John's final illness, had been used by the spirit of God to have a much more significant effect upon him than he had even cared to admit. He had been far too proud, and far too well-educated, to concede that this evangelical faith had anything whatsoever to do with him. Was it not, after all, by and large, the masses of the common people who flocked to hear revolutionary preachers like Whitefield? And Wesley? And even that man in Olney, Newton?

After ten days John had recovered sufficiently to allow William to return to Olney, and Orchard Side, convinced that his brother was well on the way to health again.

On 16th February, 1770, William was once more summoned, by an urgent letter, to visit John. His brother was ill again. So ill, indeed, that 'the physicians entertained little hopes of his recovery'.

As he journeyed to Cambridge, William was challenged by his brother's obviously deteriorating physical condition, and his ultimate destiny, should he die without Christ.

Regardless of the cool reception the message would no doubt be afforded, he would have to speak to John. And soon. It was his duty, he felt.

On the day following his arrival, he asked his sick brother for permission to pray with him. John consented to this request, and William was delighted.

The ice was broken!

He was soon to discover, though, that although a crack had appeared in the ice, John's heart was still frozen. Solid. As far as the gospel was concerned.

For days he prayed with his brother, and told him earnestly of the love of his Saviour. But the ill man appeared as careless as ever. Totally disinterested.

Five days after William had arrived to be with his brother, John was seized by a violent attack of asthma. William sat by his bedside all day, praying for him. When he assured John that others were praying for him too, (for they were, especially back in Olney), his gasping-for-breath brother replied, " That is true, and I hope God will have mercy upon me".

In his own written account of John's conversion, William describes a conversation which he had with his brother, later on that same day :-

> "At night when he was quite worn out with the fatigue of labouring for breath and could get no rest, his asthma still continuing, he turned to me and said with a melancholy air, 'Brother, I seem marked out for misery, you know some people are so-.' That moment I felt my

heart enlarged and such a persuasion of the love of God to him was wrought in my soul that I replied with confidence, and as if I had authority given me to say it, 'But that is not your case, you are marked out for mercy.'"

On Saturday, 10th March, William entered his ill brother's bedroom, to find John with his eyes closed in prayer. Suddenly he burst into tears and said with a loud cry, "Oh, forsake me not!"

After speaking to him briefly, William crept silently from the room. He realized what was happening.

John was having a personal experience with God.

When he went back into the bedroom, about an hour later, he was overjoyed at what John had to say. It was thrilling. All the prayers had been answered.

William describes it thus :-

"When I returned, he threw his arm about my neck and leaning his head against mine, he said, 'Brother, if I live, you and I shall be more like one another than we have been, but whether I live or not, all is well and will be so. I know it will. I have felt that which I never felt before and am sure that God has visited me with this sickness to teach me what I was too proud to learn in health. I never had satisfaction until now. The doctrines I had been used to referred me to myself for the foundation of my hopes and then I could find nothing to rest upon: the sheet anchor of the soul was wanting. I thought you wrong yet wished to believe as you did. I found myself unable to believe yet always thought I should one day be brought to do so. You suffered more than I have done before you believed these truths, but our sufferings, though different in their kind and measure, were directed to the same end.

*I hope He has taught me that which He teaches none but
His own. I hope so. These things were foolishness to me
once, but now I have a firm foundation and am satisfied.'"*

After that conversion experience, John's physical condition
seemed to improve for a few days. He was full of the joy of
the Lord and resting in a wonderful peace of mind and soul
which he had never known before. He even expressed a longing to pay a last visit to Olney to see the river yet again, but
more importantly to 'spend an hour with Mr. Newton',
talking over the things of God.

What a transformation!

Unfortunately, however, John was not able to fulfil his
desire.

Late in the afternoon of March 14th, his condition became
suddenly worse. He was obviously weaker in body and his
speech became rambling and faltering. The patient appeared
to realize himself that his strength and power to reason were
ebbing away.

Addressing William, who rarely left his side, one day, he
said, weakly, "Well, while I have any senses left, my thoughts
will be poured out in the praise of God! I have an interest in
Christ, in His blood and sufferings, and my sins are forgiven
me. Have I not cause to praise Him? When my understanding fails me, as I think it will soon, then He will pity my weak-
ness!"

On the day before he died, during a period of severe and
continual pain, he summoned up enough strength to give his
anxious brother a faint smile, and whisper, "Brother, I am as
happy as a king!"

Early next morning William was called to his brother's bedside. He found that his brother had lapsed into unconscious-
ness. He lay perfectly still. Free at last from pain.

Probably sensing that the end was near, and that it would be unbearably distressing for the sensitive poet to be present, the nurses prevailed upon him to leave the room.

Five minutes later John Cowper passed away. Passed on. Passed over, to be with Christ.

William was deeply upset, but not quite as deeply as he would have been had John not come to faith in Christ. This was his 'strong consolation'.

The letter he wrote to his aunt, Mrs Madan, on the Saturday following John's death, sums up his sentiments precisely:-

Dear Aunt,

You may possibly by this time have heard of the Death of my dear Brother. I should not have left you to learn of it from any but myself, had I either spirits or opportunity to write sooner. He died on Tuesday last, the 20th.

It was not judged proper that I should attend the funeral. I therefore took leave of the melancholy scene as soon as possible, and returned to Olney on Thursday.He has left me to sing of Mercy and Judgment. Greater suffrings than he underwent are seldom seen, Greater Mercy than he received, I believe never. His views of Gospel Grace were as clear, and his sense of his Interest in Christ, as strong, as if he had been exercised in the Christian walk and warfare many years. This is my consolation, and strong consolation I find it, that he is gone to his Father and my Father, to his God and my God...

> *I am, Dear Aunt,*
>> *Yours affectionately in the Lord,*
>>> *Wm. Cowper.*

Olney.
March 24th 1770.

17

'A Bustle Within!'

❖

ON HIS RETURN FROM CAMBRIDGE, THE SENSITIVE
MIND OF WILLIAM COWPER WAS PLAGUED BY MIXED
EMOTIONS.

He was comforted by the knowledge that his brother had
trusted in Christ before his death, and was therefore in heaven.
That, at least, was some consolation.

On the other hand, however, a deepening sense of depression seemed to invade his peace of mind. John's passing, in
addition to depriving him of his only brother, had brought
him again face to face with the reality of death

And death, whether in Christ or out of Christ, was still
death.

The last earthly farewell.

On previous occasions when William Cowper had experienced death at close quarters he had become unbalanced. It
was then that he had attempted suicide himself.

This sense of gloom often led him to long for the joy and happiness that he had enjoyed, 'when first he knew the Lord'.

In a hymn, written at that time and entitled, 'The Contrite Heart', based on the words of Isaiah 57 v 15, he opens the door just a chink, allowing us to share the coldness and flatness of his state of mind and soul :-

The Lord will happiness divine,
  On contrite hearts bestow :
Then tell me, gracious God, is mine,
  A contrite heart, or no?

I hear, but seem to hear in vain,
  Insensible as steel ;
If ought is felt, 'tis only pain,
  To find I cannot feel.

I sometimes think myself inclin'd
  To love thee, if I could ;
But often feel another mind,
  Averse to all that's good.

My best desires are faint and few,
  I fain would strive for more ;
But when I cry, "My strength renew,"
  Seem weaker than before.

Thy saints are comforted I know,
  And love thy house of pray'r ;
I therefore go where others go,
  But find no comfort there.

O make this heart rejoice, or ache,
  Decide this doubt for me ;
And if it be not broken, break,
  And heal it, if it be.

(Olney Hymns. Book 1. Hymn 64.)

This hymn could possibly be better described as a POEM of personal doubt and conflict than a SONG of praise and worship. It would be difficult to imagine how it could have a very edifying or encouraging effect on a group of Christians assembled in the middle of a hassled week for their Prayer and Bible study session!

Although his friends sought to reassure him and lift his spirits in the months following upon John's death, Cowper was often afflicted by periods of doubt and spiritual turmoil.

In March, 1771, John and Mary Newton went to London on business and John wrote back to Olney, describing to William and Mary Unwin the hurly-burly and distraction the great city.

In his reply to that letter Cowper confided:-

'... If you find yourself hinder'd by an Outside Bustle, I am equally hinder'd by a Bustle within; the Lord I trust will give Peace in his own time, but I can truly say that for the most part my Soul is amongst Lions ...'

and later in the same letter he bemoans his lack of mental stability, and Christian contentment:-

'.... neither on Tuesday Night at the Meeting, nor on the Sabbath was my Burthen removed. I got Paul's Answer I trust, 'My grace shall be sufficient for thee', but was not, like him, content with it...'

His three close companions were all perturbed by William's frequent bouts of depression, and each tried to help remedy the situation in his or her own peculiar way.

Mary Newton sought to counter his gloominess with her cheerfulness. His hopelessness with her hopefulness. This was more than just a 'look on the sunny side of life' philosophy, though. It was a genuine attempt to encourage her friend in the riches that were his through faith in Christ Jesus.

It rarely worked.

Mary Unwin, housekeeper and confidante, was a source of stability to the fickle poet. She had always a calming influence. And a word of counsel from the stable foundation of her deep-rooted Christian faith.

Her proposed contribution to the improvement of the mental and spiritual condition of William Cowper was impelled by two factors. One external. The other of the heart.

In the summer of 1772, her daughter Susanna had become engaged to be married to Matthew Powley, an evangelical minister. Mary reasoned, and probably with some justification, that the gossiping tongues which had wagged so incessantly in Olney when Squire Cowper, as they called him, was living in Orchard Side with two unattached women, would wag ten times harder when he was living with only one!

The second reason was deeper. Altogether more personal. Of the heart rather than the head.

Although she was older than Cowper, having lived in the same house as the man for the past seven years, she had come to share in his innermost thoughts. If anybody knew him, she did. And she really liked him. To say that she loved him might be overstating it, but she was certainly filled with maternal concern for her intellectually brilliant but spiritually shaky companion.

Having given due consideration to these matters, she, or they, decided therefore, in the autumn of 1772 that they also should be married. And so they were engaged. 'Betrothed', they called it.

It was arranged that the marriage would take place in the spring of the next year. March or April 1773.

Tidy things up nicely.

John Newton, too, had given much thought to ways in which he could help his ailing friend, and he came up with a couple of schemes. To occupy the over-productive brain of the poet. And at the same time help him develop profitably in his love of, and service for, God.

They were good ideas, he felt.

All that remained was for him to seek to implement them...

18

The Worth Of Prayer

❖

JOHN NEWTON WAS A FIRM BELIEVER IN PRAYER.
AND IN THE VALUE OF PRAYER. HIS HYMN ON THE
SUBJECT, ENTITLED, 'THE POWER OF PRAYER',
WOULD DEMONSTRATE THAT HE COULD NOT ONLY
ILLUSTRATE THIS THEME WITH BIBLE ANECDOTES
BUT ALSO THAT HE HAD EXPERIENCED THE REALITY
OF IT IN THE UPS-AND-DOWNS OF DAY-TO-DAY
LIVING.

> In themselves, as weak as worms,
> How can poor believers stand ;
> When temptations, foes, and storms,
> Press them close on ev'ry hand?
>
> Weak, indeed, they feel they are,
> But they know the throne of grace ;
> And the God, who answers prayer,
> Helps them when they seek his face.

Tho' the Lord awhile delay,
Succour they at length obtain ;
He who taught their hearts to pray,
Will not let them cry in vain.

Wrestling prayer can wonders do,
Bring relief in deepest straits ;
Prayer can force a passage thro'
Iron bars and brazen gates.

Hezekiah on his knees
Proud Assyrias' host subdued ;
And when smitten with disease,
Had his life by prayer renewed.

Peter, tho' confined and chained,
Prayer prevailed and brought him out ;
When Elijah prayed, it rained,
After three long years of drought.

We can likewise witness bear,
That the Lord is still the same ;
Tho' we feared he would not hear,
Suddenly deliverance came.

For the wonders he has wrought,
Let us now our praises give ;
And by sweet experience taught,
Call upon him while we live.

(Olney Hymns. Book2. Hymn 61.)

The first way in which Newton considered that he could
help his friend was to encourage him to become more actively

involved in the spiritual life of the local community. He encouraged William to take part in the prayer meetings in the Great House and to accompany him when he went to visit the sick.

More outward spiritual participation would surely help him to overcome his inward natural reticence, he reasoned. Bring him 'out of himself.' And at the same time use his innate tenderness and close contact with God, for the benefit of others.

And so the congregation at the mid-week prayer session began to hear the voice of William Cowper interceding with God for them in prayer. Such was his command of the language and commitment of faith that everyone was thrilled to hear him pray.

Newton said that he spoke, "as if he saw the Lord whom he addressed face to face." Someone from the town, reflecting years later on William Cowper's stay in Olney, summed up the reaction of many when he remarked, "Of all the men I ever heard pray, no one equalled Mr. Cowper."

Whilst others appreciated 'the awful yet delightful consciousness of the presence of the Saviour', that attended the shy poet's prayers, these public appearances had an effect on the man himself. Although nobody would ever have guessed it when he stood up to lead in prayer, he confessed that, "my mind was always greatly agitated for some hours preceding." Describing his own reserved nature once, he said, "I am amongst those to whom a public exhibition of themselves on any occasion is mortal poison."

It is little wonder then, that when he wrote a hymn which he called, 'Exhortation to Prayer', for the meeting in The Great House, he mentioned the

'various hindrances we meet,
In coming to a mercy seat.'

He, like all of us, had been taught and was convinced, that,

'Satan trembles when he sees,
The weakest saint upon his knees.'

Like all of us, he had also experienced the struggle it is sometimes to get alone with God in prayer, but he had also enjoyed the blessings that are showered upon the Christian lives of those who make the effort to spend time on their knees.

Those who make prayer a way of life.

His hymn is still in use in some hymn-books today :-

What various hindrances we meet
In coming to a mercy-seat?
Yet who that knows the worth of prayer,
But wishes to be often there.

Prayer makes the dark'ned cloud withdraw,
Prayer climbs the ladder Jacob saw ;
Gives exercise to faith and love,
Brings ev'ry blessing from above.

Restraining prayer, we cease to fight ;
Prayer makes the Christian's armour bright ;
And Satan trembles, when he sees
The weakest saint upon his knees.

While Moses stood with arms spread wide,
Success was found on Israel's side (e) ;
But when thro' weariness they failed,
That moment Amalek prevailed.

Have you no words? Ah, think again!
Words flow apace when you complain ;
And fill your fellow-creature's ear
With the sad tale of all your care.

Were half the breath thus vainly spent,
To heaven in supplication sent ;
Your cheerful song would oftener be,
"Hear what the Lord has done for me!"
(Olney Hymns. Book 2. Hymn 60)
(e) Exodus 17. 11.

'Prayer makes the darkened cloud withdraw.'
Had John Newton's idea been a good one?
Had 'the darkened clouds' of doubt, of depression, of despondency, really withdrawn? Had they gone away to stay away? For good?
Or would they just come drifting back on the next wind of adversity?

19

Pillow Lace

❖

THE MAIN OCCUPATION OF THE PEOPLE OF OLNEY IN THE 18TH CENTURY WAS LACE-MAKING. THE WOMEN, WELL OVER ONE THOUSAND OF THEM, WERE ENGAGED IN THE SKILFUL AND INTRICATE MANUFACTURE OF PILLOW LACE, SO CALLED BECAUSE IT WAS MADE OVER A PILLOW WHICH THE COTTAGER HELD ON HER KNEE OR IN A 'THREE-LEGGED PILLOW HORSE' IN FRONT OF HER. NOT BECAUSE IT WAS USED EXCLUSIVELY FOR THE TRIMMING OF PILLOWS. FOR IT WASN'T.

It was one of the activities engaged in by these lace-makers that prompted John Newton to consider another activity in which both he and his constant, but often disconsolate, companion, William Cowper, could co-operate.

The lace-making tradition in Olney had begun in the previous two centuries when Protestant Flemish lace-makers had fled to England to escape persecution because of their faith. On arrival in Engand these highly skilled craftsmen and women settled in Bedfordshire, Buckinghamshire and Nottinghamshire and began to ply their trade. It is interesting to note that these immigrants brought more than their lace and the ability to produce it, with them into the land of their adoption. Cabbages, carrots and celery all arrived in Britain with Flanders lace!

Most authorities on the subject refer to Olney as being the centre of the Buckinghamshire Point Lace industry.

Daniel Defoe, who made his 'Tours' in 1684 and published his account of them in 1724, speaks about "much bone lace being made in Ouldney," and "veils and other lace of the finer sorts being made."

Lace was woven in two different locations. In the cottages and in the lace-schools.

In the schools, the girls of the town, and a very few boys, were instructed in the finer points of the craft by experienced lacemakers. These children sat over their pillows in which they deftly placed the pattern-making pins, for long hours each day. When the pins were in place they used a set of bobbins, usually twenty-four, to weave the delicate lace.

In summer, when it was warm and bright, lessons were held outdoors. This was quite pleasant. There was always something to see. Some diversion or other.

Winter, however, was a different story. Working conditions were tough. It was usually very cold in the schools since no fires could be lit as smoke or dust would darken the lace. The only heat the girls had was a 'Dicky Pot'. This fire-pot was made of rough brown ware and the pupils had them filled with hot wood ashes from the baker's every morning for a farthing. In school, this pot, placed on the floor, kept the feet and legs warm. That is until somebody set her petticoats on fire! Then there was a whole fuss!

Not only was it cold in winter. It was also dark. Light in school on dull days, and in the cottages on dark winter evenings, was provided by a candle-stool. This was a taller-than-usual three or four-legged stool with a tall candle in the centre of it. In holes around the candle were inverted bottles of "snow water". These flasks of water focused the light from the candle on to the lacemakers' pillows. Often there were two, and sometimes even three, circles of weavers around one candle-stool. The more experienced workers sat closest to the light, in the first circle, and were known as First Lights, the second row were Second Lights, and so on.

To pass the time as they worked, and to help them count their pins, either at home or in lace school, the women chanted rhymes. Lace-making "tellings" or "tells", they were called.

One of the traditional Olney ones went something like this :-

"A lad down at Olney looked over a wall
And saw nineteen little golden girls playing at ball.
Golden girls, golden girls, will you be mine?
You shall neither wash dishes nor wait on the swine.
But sit on a cushion and sew a fine seam,
Eat white bread and butter and strawberries and cream."

'Nineteen' was a common number in the tells, as that was the number at which counting down started. Next verse had 'eighteen', then 'seventeen', and on and on they chanted. The 'golden girls' were the golden pins that marked out the pattern of the lace.

Some of these chants or 'tells' were also used for children's games. One of the games the children used to play was jumping over the candle-stool, trying to accomplish the feat without extinguishing the lighted candle. To achieve this in bare-feet and wearing long breeches or half-a-dozen petticoats required a lot of agility.

No wonder they chanted as they stood around, the name of the competing high-jumper being inserted in the rhyme as appropriate:-

"Jack be nimble! Jack be quick!
Jack jump over the candlestick!"

It was specifically these lacemaking 'tells' that furnished John Newton with his next idea. If these women, many of whom couldn't read, could learn the chants so easily, why could they not learn poems if he and his friend were to put Scripture passages into verse? It would be a very effective way of getting the message across. And instead of chanting meaningless rhymes as they made their lace they could recite poems-with-a-purpose. Hymns-to-be.

The lace makers of Olney would love to have their Sunday sermon in verse, he reckoned. For many of them had strong non-conformist, God-fearing, Bible-believing backgrounds. And they weren't afraid to let everyone around know it either. In their own quiet way.

Obviously one method they used to witness to others was the inscriptions which they had engraved on their bobbins. Whilst some of the weavers used quaint sayings or even the family history to personalise their bobbins, many of the Christian women used Scripture texts.

'Prepare to meet thy God' and 'Ye must be born again' were only two of many texts in common use. Two bobbins, still in existence in museums bear the inscriptions, 'Do not steel', and, 'Jesus weept'. The bobbin-makers were all master-craftsmen but they were patently not all master-spellers!

William Cowper affords us two insights into the quiet and unswerving commitment of these poverty-stricken people, one in a poem, and the other in a letter, written long afterwards.

In the poem he contrasts the simple faith of an Olney lacemaker with the teachings of Voltaire, the French philosopher, who was actively opposing the Gospel at that time :-

'Yon cottager, who weaves at her own door,
Pillow and bobbins all her little store ;
Content though mean, and cheerful if not gay,
Shuffling her threads about the livelong day,
Just earns a scanty pittance, and at night
Lies down secure, her heart and pocket light ;
She, for her humble sphere by nature fit,
Has little understanding, and no wit ;
Receives no praise, but, though her lot be such,
(Toilsome and indigent,) she renders much ;
Just knows, and knows no more, her Bible true—
A truth the brilliant Frenchman never knew.
And in that charter reads, with sparkling eyes,
Her title to a treasure in the skies.
    O happy peasant! O unhappy bard!
His the mere tinsel, hers the rich reward ;
He praised perhaps for ages ages yet to come,
She never heard of half-a-mile from home :
He lost in errors his vain heart prefers,
She safe in the simplicity of hers.
    Not many wise, rich, noble, or profound
In science, win one inch of heavenly ground :
And is it not a mortifying thought
The poor should gain it, and the rich should not?'...

(From, "Truth". 1781.)

In the letter, written in 1793, Cowper describes for a friend the devotion of these impoverished lacemakers, as demonstrated by their regular attendance at the Sunday morning prayer meeting in the Great House. :-

> *' Time was when on Sabbath mornings in the winter I rose before day, and by the light of a lanthorn trudged with Mrs Unwin, often through snow and rain, to a prayer meeting at the Great House. There I always found assembled forty or fifty poor folks who preferred a glimpse of the light of God's countenance and favour to the comforts of a warm bed, or to any comforts that the world could afford them ; and there I have often myself partaken that blessing with them.'*

So, realising that they had a ready-made and potentially very receptive audience, John Newton put a proposal to his fellow-poet and daily companion. Whether he suggested it all at one big exciting go, or whether he introduced it and talked it up, we will probably never know.

Or whether the initial suggestion came during a walk by the Ouse in the meadows around Olney, or during a chat by the fire in the parlour at Orchard Side, we will probably never know, either.

The important thing was that it came. Sometime. Somewhere.

And it was simple.

They would compile a Hymn-book. All of their own compositions.

The creative curate advanced the opinion that the time, and all the circumstances, were just ripe for such an exercise.

After all, Dr. Isaac Watts had published his, 'Hymns and Spiritual Songs'. And the Wesley brothers had their, 'Hymns and Sacred Verse'. And if those men could produce hymn-books, what was to hinder them from doing the same?.. The work of these early hymn-writers could only benefit the publication of a collection of their hymns, in that it had served as an introduction to congregational singing. Broken down barriers. Dispelled silly notions. Opened up the way.

And another thing, too... Some of Cowper's early hymns were beginning to appear, anonymously, in miscellaneous collections. That needed tidying up.

Think of the lasting spiritual blessing it would bring to the lacemakers as well! They would have a new tale to 'tell'. The Bible and the basic tenets of the Christian faith. All in easy-to-remember verse.

When the let's-produce-an-Olney-hymnbook proposal was put to the one for whose overall benefit the whole scheme was hatched in the first instance, William Cowper, in 1771, he was pleased. Maybe not jumping-up-and-down excited, but pleased. It would, he admitted, fulfil two ambitions for him.

It would afford him a genuine opportunity for spiritual service, a medium through which he could communicate his faith to others.

And it would satisfy what he called his, "modest literary ambition".

Having gained his friend's approval of, and promise of co-operation in, the writing of hymns for the initial use of the lacemakers of Olney and the eventual use of the Christian world at large, John Newton realised that there was no to time to waste.

If the gathering gloom around William Cowper was to be dispelled, and his poetic genius displayed, there was no time to spare.

They would have to get to work at once. Immediately. Straight away.

20

'Looking Unto Jesus'

❖

SOON BOTH MEN BECAME ENTHUSIASTIC ABOUT THIS NEW PROJECT.

The best place to make a start would be the mid-week meeting in the Great House, they decided. The people who attended there were keen. Hungry for the Word.

They could both appreciate that this venture had great potential. For God, and the spread of His Gospel. For the congregation at Olney, and their spiritual development. And last, but not least, for themselves. For the employment of their poetic gift, the deepening of their natural friendship, and the enhancement of their Christian lives. It would serve to draw them, each as an individual, into closer communion with the Lord.

So they set to work with a will. Writing hymns, or poems for chorus speaking and group instruction, as they were essentially at first.

How would they be received?

That remained to be seen.

Many of the hymns that proceeded from both men, in those early days, were hymns of testimony. Neither writer had ever lost the sense of wonder at what God had done for him, and each was able to express the marvel of God's grace to him with genuine sincerity.

It was easy for them. They lived so close to it.

Two such hymns follow. In each, the author rejoices in the blessings of salvation and states his desire to live close to the Saviour. And to see more of Him.

The first one, by William Cowper, entitled, 'My Soul Thirsteth for God', still survives in some hymnbooks until this present day :-

> I thirst, but not as once I did,
> The vain delights of earth to share ;
> Thy wounds, EMMANUEL, all forbid,
> That I should seek my pleasures there.

> It was the sight of thy dear cross,
> First weaned my soul from earthly things ;
> And taught me to esteem as dross,
> The mirth of fools and pomp of kings.

> I want that grace that springs from thee,
> That quickens all things where it flows ;
> And makes a wretched thorn, like me,
> Bloom as the myrtle, or the rose.

> Dear fountain of delight unknown !
> No longer sink below the brim ;
> But overflow, and pour me down
> A living, and life-giving stream !

For sure, of all the plants that share
The notice of thy Father's eye ;
None proves less grateful to his care,
Or yields him meaner fruit than I.

(Olney Hymns. Book 3. Hymn 61.)

The next hymn, from the pen of John Newton, doesn't seem to have made it to wide usage in current hymnals. Yet it is beautiful. Based on the theme of "Looking unto Jesus", Hebrews 12 v.2, it gives us a glimpse beyond the business-like exterior of the converted ex-seaman, right into the warmth of his soul. Revealing the secret of his inner strength :-

By various maxims, forms and rules,
That pass for wisdom in the schools,
I strove my passion to restrain ;
But all my efforts proved in vain.

But since the Saviour I have known,
My rules are all reduced to one ;
To keep my Lord, by faith, in view,
This strength supplies and motives too.

I see him lead a suff'ring life,
Patient, amidst reproach and strife ;
And from his pattern courage take
To bear, and suffer, for his sake.

Upon the cross I see him bled,
And by the sight from guilt am freed ;
This sight destroys the life of sin,
And quickens heavenly life within.

To look to JESUS as he rose
Confirms my faith, disarms my foes ;
Satan I shame and overcome,
By pointing to my Saviour's tomb.

Exalted on his glorious throne,
I see him make my cause his own ;
Then all my anxious cares subside,
For JESUS lives, and will provide.

I see him look with pity down,
And hold in view the conqu'rors' crown ;
If pressed with griefs and cares before,
My soul revives, nor asks for more.

By faith I see the hour at hand
When in his presence I shall stand ;
Then it will be my endless bliss,
To see him where, and as, he is.

(Olney Hymns. Book 1. Hymn 134.)

With such a grasp of Scriptural truth, set forth in a self-abasing, Christ-exalting manner, the Great House mid-week meeting regulars, too, began to appreciate the value of the easy-learning, take-it-home-in-your-head approach.

It seemed to be a good idea.

Worth developing...

21

'Faith's Review And Expectation'

❖

THE TWO YEARS, 1771-1772, WERE TO PROVE THE MOST PRODUCTIVE YEARS OF THE PARTNERSHIP OF COWPER & NEWTON (HYMNWRITERS).

Many conversations, no doubt, took place during those days. There would have been many crossings of the Guinea Orchard, both by day and night. Many walks to and through the surrounding villages. Long hours spent by the fireside.

Each man would read, or perhaps recite, to his friend, the latest poem he had composed. It would then be discussed, at some length. Evaluated for both its poetic qualities and spiritual worth.

A decision would also have to be taken as to when it could most suitably and effectively be presented at the Great House. To a gradually-getting-used to it and finding-a-lot-of-use for it, congregation.

Well over one third of the hymns that emanated from this hymn-writing confederacy were based on verses from the Bible. These were used as the text for the sermon, or message. Then, at some stage in the address, the poem, or hymn, was introduced to expand the thought and summarise the content.

And everybody learnt it!

Or tried to learn it!

Or was supposed to try to learn it!

This allowed the lacemakers, for whom learning-by-heart was a way of life, to 'tell' the story the next day. And the next. And the next...

The first we will consider is by William Cowper, and was based on a verse from the book by the prophet Zechariah :-

"In that day there shall be a fountain opened to the house of David and to the   inhabitants of Jerusalem for sin and for uncleanness." (Chapter 13 v.1)

Cowper entitled his work, 'Praise for the Fountain Opened.'

You will probably have sung it. Or at least heard it sung. Somewhere. At some time or another :-

> There is a fountain filled with blood
>   Drawn from EMMANUEL's veins ;
> And sinners, plunged beneath that flood,
>   Loose all their guilty stains.
>
> The dying thief rejoiced to see
>   That fountain in his day ;
> And there have I, as vile as he,
>   Washed all my sins away.
>
> Dear dying Lamb, thy precious blood
>   Shall never loose its power ;
> Till all the ransomed church of God
>   Be saved to sin no more.

E'er since, by faith, I saw the stream
Thy flowing wounds supply :
Redeeming love has been my theme,
And shall be till I die.

Then in a nobler sweeter song
I'll sing thy power to save ;
When this poor lisping, stamm'ring tongue
Lies silent in the grave.

LORD, I believe thou hast prepared
(Unworthy tho' I be)
For me a blood-bought free reward,
A golden harp for me !

'Tis strung, and tuned, for endless years,
And formed by power divine ;
To sound, in God the Father's ears,
No other name but thine.

(Olney Hymns. Book 1. Hymn 79.)

It is interesting to observe that this well-known hymn is also a hymn of testimony. It is written, as are so many of Cowper's, in the first person singular. Ever aware of his own unworthiness, he still rejoices that he has had his sins washed away, and that he will, one day, beyond the grave, sing of Christ's "power to save".

The progressive theme of what was to become one of John Newton's most famous hymns is much the same as that of 'Praise for the Fountain Opened'. What God, in His grace, has done, is doing, and will yet do, in the life of the believer. Though not as obviously autobiographical as, 'In Evil Long I took Delight', it still contains unmistakable references to his early life and experiences.

It all began one evening when the curate took as his text the opening words of David's prayer in 1 Chronicles chapter 17 :-

> *"And David the king came and sat before the Lord, and said, Who am I, O LORD God, and what is mine house, that thou hast brought me hitherto?*
> *And yet this was a small thing in thine eyes, O God ; for thou hast also spoken of thy servant's house for a great while to come, and hast regarded me according to the estate of a man of high degree, O LORD God."*

Then he explained to his audience how that David had come to this point in his life. Praising God for His care. His mercy and forgiveness. His provision for the future.

And all of that to one so insignificant. So unworthy.

Reflecting upon the preserving grace of God to him in his turbulent seafaring days, and having, perhaps, rolling over and over in the back of his mind, the words of Cowper's, 'Song of Mercy and Judgment' which had been written some nine years earlier, and with which he would probably have been familiar, John Newton wrote a poem for that meeting. To illustrate the gist of his message.

He called it, 'Faith's Review and Expectation.'

It went like this :-

> Amazing grace! (how sweet the sound)
>   That saved a wretch like me!
> I once was lost, but now am found,
>   Was blind, but now I see.
>
> 'Twas grace that taught my heart to fear,
>   And grace my fears relieved ;
> How precious did that grace appear,
>   The hour I first believed!

Thro' many dangers, toils and snares,
  I have already come ;
'Tis grace has brought me safe thus far,
  And grace will lead me home.

The Lord has promised good to me,
  His word my hope secures ;
He will my shield and portion be,
  As long as life endures.

Yes, when this flesh and heart shall fail,
  And mortal life shall cease ;
I shall possess, within the vail,
  A life of joy and peace.

The earth shall soon dissolve like snow,
  The sun forbear to shine ;
But God, who called me here below,
  Will be for ever mine.

       (Olney Hymns. Book 1. Hymn 41.)

As he presented his latest hymn to the congregation that evening, neither the author of it, or those who learnt it off, verse by verse, could have had the slightest inkling as to how God, in His wonderful wisdom, was set to use this simple song about His amazing grace, in the years to come.

Although written in a small English town, this hymn was initially not well known in England, and does not appear in any of the earlier hymnbooks.

It was in America that it became established.

The Americans did two things for it. The first was that they set it to the tune of an old plantation melody entitled, 'Loving Lambs'. That tune is the one we now know so well as, 'Amazing Grace.' Without question a worthwhile contribution and one that has in some measure led to the popularity of the hymn.

The other change to Newton's poem, made in America, was the substitution of,

> 'When we've been there ten thousand years
> Bright shining as the sun,
> We've no less days to sing God's praise
> Than when we first begun.'

for the original last verse.

Whether this alternative final verse, which first appeared in 1859, is actually an improvement on Newton's, must be, of necessity, a matter of personal opinion.

In the 1970's 'Amazing Grace' was top of the Hit Parade. The plaintive skirl of the bagpipes immortalised the tune and constant daily exposure on radio, T.V., and even juke-box, had the words on everybody's lips.

Many Christians were shocked by this. Others, who saw it as a means used by God to promote the Gospel, were thrilled.

Two hundred years earlier, in the 1770's, the church-going residents of Olney, to whom Pops were short, sharp, explosive sounds that they had never even dreamed of trying to get to the Top of, had sat in flickering light learning this poem by their verse-making curate.

As he read it out from his quill-written copy they repeated it.

Word by word. Line by line. Then verse by verse...

How wonderful, how marvellous, how amazing, are the ways and works of God!

22

Letters And Titles

❖

THE SEA-CAPTAIN WHO HAD KEPT DETAILED AND
SYSTEMATIC LOGS ON BOARD HIS VESSELS
AND WHO HAD CONDUCTED REGULAR SUNDAY
SERVICES WITH HIS CREWS, WAS A MAN OF ORDER.

He liked to plan well ahead. Know what he was doing.
Why he was doing it. And how, eventually, he hoped to achieve
it.

It was inevitable that he should carry that sense of struc-
ture over into his work as curate of Olney.

In addition to being a man with an ordered mind John Newton was also a serious student of the Bible. Both he, and his
highly-educated friend, had more than just an, ' I-don't-know-
but-the-experts-tell-us', acquaintance with both Hebrew and
Greek . They were experts.

Appreciating the potential value of a methodical expos-
ition of the Scriptures to his congregation, he must have, at

some time during those busy but fruitful preach-it, teach-it, and then-write-a-hymn-about-it days, embarked upon such a venture. Not only would the teaching have been beneficial to his audiences, but the exercise of study and preparation of such subjects would also have been beneficial to William Cowper, the intense Christian with the classical education.

There is evidence that the poet and the preacher engaged in at least two joint enterprises of this nature.

One had its origins in the Old Testament.

The other was from the New.

The New Testament series of lessons was based on 'The Churches in Asia', Revelation, chapters 2 and 3. Hymns were written on five of the seven letters to the churches. Four of these were by Newton himself, and one, that on the letter to the church in Sardis, was Cowper's.

These hymns, or poems, were not the best or most-enduring of the writings that the two men ever produced. But being, as they were, almost direct paraphrases of the relevant Scripture passages, they served the purpose for which they were intended.

Implanting the Word of God into the hearts and minds of the largely illiterate, but spiritually and mentally active congregation in Olney.

The theme of the Old Testament teaching was the Hebrew titles of God. Jehovah. The bulk of this work, whether he volunteered to do it, or had it suggested or even assigned to him, was by William Cowper, who wrote six poems. Each was on a separate O.T. title of Jehovah, as follows:-

JEHOVAH-JIREH. The Lord will provide. Genesis 22 v.14.

JEHOVAH-ROPHI. I am the Lord that healeth thee. Exodus 15 v.26.

JEHOVAH-NISSI. The Lord my banner. Exodus 17 v.15.

JEHOVAH-SHALOM. The Lord send peace. Judges 6 v.24.

JEHOVAH-TSIDKENU. The Lord our righteousness. Jeremiah 23 v.6.

JEHOVAH-SHAMMAH. The Lord is there. Ezekiel 48 v.35. Whether written at the same time, and for the same series of studies, or at some later date for another occasion, it is impossible to tell, but John Newton also wrote a rather lengthy hymn on the subject, JEHOVAH-JIREH. The Lord will provide.

Selected verses of this hymn are to be found in some of the older hymnbooks. Perhaps it was considered too long for a total inclusion.

Here it is, as Newton penned it :-

> Tho' troubles assail
> And dangers affright,
> Tho' friends should all fail
> And foes all unite ;
> Yet one thing secures us,
> Whatever betide,
> The Scripture assures us,
> "The Lord will provide."

> The birds, without barn
> Or storehouse are fed,
> From them let us learn
> To trust for our bread ;
> His saints, what is fitting,
> Shall ne'er be denied,
> So long as 'tis written,
> "The Lord will provide."

> We may, like the ships,
> By tempests be tossed

On perilous deeps,
But cannot be lost.
Tho' Satan enrages
The wind and the tide,
The promise engages,
"The Lord will provide."

His call we obey
Like Abram of old,
Not knowing our way,
But faith makes us bold ;
For tho' we are strangers
We have a good Guide,
And trust in all dangers,
"The Lord will provide."

When Satan appears
To stop up our path,
And fill us with fears,
We triumph by faith ;
He cannot take from us,
Tho' oft he has tried,
This heart-cheering promise,
"The Lord will provide."

He tells us we're weak,
Our hope is in vain,
The good that we seek
We shall never obtain ;
But when such suggestions
Our spirits have plied,
This answers all questions,
"The Lord will provide."

No strength of our own,
Or goodness we claim,
Yet since we have known
The Saviour's great name ;
In this our strong tower
For safety we hide,
The Lord is our power,
"The Lord will provide."

When life sinks apace
And death is in view,
This word of his grace
Shall comfort us thro' :
No fearing or doubting
With Christ on our side,
We hope to die shouting,
"The Lord will provide!"

(Olney Hymns. Book1. Hymn 7.)

The nautical imagery of the third verse is interesting. John Newton could write with genuine conviction about ships. And storms. And perilous deeps. He had been there. Had first-hand experience.

The short crisp lines of the composition and expected-repetition of the last line of each stanza would make for easy learning.

So whilst the production of a-hymn-a-week for the Great House was not only appreciated by the audiences and a spur to spiritual involvement for the two authors, it was also encouraging them to experiment with poetic style. As the theme and situation lent itself.

Valuable experience for the future.

23

'Clear Shining After Rain'

❖

UNFORTUNATELY, NEITHER THE BONHOMIE OF MARY NEWTON, THE PROSPECT OF MARRIAGE TO MARY UNWIN, OR THE LET'S-WALK-AND-TALK-AND-PRAY-AND-WRITE THERAPY OF JOHN NEWTON SEEMED TO EFFECT ANY LASTING IMPROVEMENT UPON WILLAM COWPER'S MORBID STATE OF MIND.

The dark clouds of depression continued to gather. Occasionally, welcome shafts of sunlight punctuated the gloom, providing warming rays of hope for everyone.

It was like nursing a relative who is chronically ill. When the patient appears brighter, the carers have a lighter heart. But when the ailing one has a bad day, a sombre shadow falls over everybody.

So it was with the faithful three, who daily waited upon the unpredictable mood swings of the spiritually ardent, and mentally brilliant but rather unstable, poet.

No one was more aware of the extremes of his mental condition than Cowper himself. He oscillated between anguish and ecstacy. But there was no set or forseeable pattern to it all.

It just happened.

He illustrates his personal recognition of his own mental and spiritual state in a letter which he wrote to his aunt, Mrs. Madan, on Tuesday, 9th June, 1772. In it he says:-

> *"... At such times of spiritual distress, I am forced to account it a great matter if I can groan out something a little like a prayer for myself. I bless God I can say, 'I know in Whom I have believed!' and am persuaded He will keep me. But together with this persuasion which one would think would smooth the roughest road of life and make a paradise of a desert, I have temptations that are almost ever present with me and shed a thick gloom upon all my prospect...The Lord who chose me in the furnace of affliction is pleased to afford the tempter a large permission to try me : ..."*

Later in that same letter, and perhaps thinking that he had painted too black a picture, we see the chink in the clouds through which the sunlight streams upon the scene. Before concluding his letter, he confessed :-

> *"...But let me not conceal my Master's goodness. I have other days in my calendar. Days that would be foolishly exchanged for all the monarchies of earth! That part of the wilderness I walk through is a romantic scene. There is but little level ground in it, but mountains hard to ascend, deep and dark valleys, wild forests, caves, and dens in abundance— but when I can hear my Lord invite me from afar and say, 'Come to me my spouse, come from the*

Lebanon, from the top of Amana, from the lions' dens,
from the mountains and   the leopards,' (Song of Songs
4. 8), then I can reply with cheerfulness, 'Behold, I come
unto thee for thou art the Lord my God.'.."

So there were 'other days' in his calendar.

Days of close communion with God.

Days that evoked a cascade of praise from his lips. And from his pen.

Days when he was almost, to use Wordsworth's phrase, 'surprised by joy'.

Was he ever, sitting in his accustomed seat in 'Newton's gallery' in the church, surprised by a light of confidence and security as he sang?

Or did he ever find his own heart lifted in a personal song of praise to God for His kindness and care? Almost in spite of himself?

Perhaps he did.

Something we do know for sure is that on one occasion, and most probably on a brighter day, one of 'the other days' in his 'calendar', when he was revelling in happy harmony with God, he wrote a glad hymn of praise.

Cowper called this hymn, 'Joy and Peace in Believing', and in it he weaves his way beautifully through a series of Scripture references to the world of nature.

The 'light, that surprises the Christian while he sings' is, of course, 'the Sun of righteousness', the Lord, who rises with often-much-needed 'healing in his wings'.

Having often experienced, no doubt, on his walks around Olney, the clear quality of the air after a shower, he borrows King David's phrase from his 'last words' speech, and refers to 'clear shining after rain'.(2 Samuel 23 v. 4). And from the Saviour's example in the Gospels, of God's provision for us, as illustrated in His attention-to-detail in familiar things like flowers that grow and birds that fly, Cowper skips back to a poetic restatement of Habakkuk's avowal of confidence in God.

How it must have cheered the hearts of John Newton and the two Marys when he read it to them for their approval, before presenting it in the Great House :-

> Sometimes a light surprizes
>   The Christian while he sings ;
> It is the Lord who rises
>   With healing in his wings :
> When comforts are declining,
>   He grants the soul again
> A season of clear shining
>   To cheer it after rain.
>
> In holy contemplation,
>   We sweetly then pursue
> The theme of God's salvation,
>   And find it ever new :
> Set free from present sorrow,
>   We cheeerfully can say,
> Ee'n let the unknown to-morrow (k),
>   Bring with it what it may.
>
> It can bring with it nothing
>   But he will bear us thro' ;
> Who gives the lilies clothing
>   Will clothe his people too :
> Beneath the spreading heavens,
>   No creature but is fed ;
> And he who feeds the ravens,
>   Will give his children bread.

Though vine, nor fig-tree neither (l),
　　Their wonted fruit should bear,
Tho' all the fields should wither,
　　Nor flocks, nor herds, be there :
Yet God the same abiding,
　　His praise shall tune my voice ;
For while in him confiding,
　　I cannot but rejoice.

(k) Matthew 6 v.34　(l) Habakkuk 3 vs.17,18.
(Olney Hymns. Book 3. Hymn 48.)

John Newton was not subject to the same temperamental fluctuations as his friend ,William. He considered it, indeed, a vital part of his ministry to be available for his shy companion. To comfort and advise him at any time. So he couldn't afford to be fickle.

And anyway, there was so much to be done. And so much for which to praise God.

The rapid spread of the evangelical Christian faith in England led to him writing many letters to the leading churchmen of the period. Instructing. Advising. Debating.

Then there were the poor people of Olney to think about, many of them living well below the breadline. Just scraping a living from their lace. A kind friend of Newton's, a prosperous businessman called John Thornton, had pledged the caring curate, 'the sum of two hundred pounds a year', to help him alleviate the misery 'of the poor and needy'. This had to be distributed. And it required time. And tact.

Always at the back of his mind too, there was the proposed hymn-book. Every hymn either he or William C. wrote he logged away. For future inclusion in what was intended as their joint publication.

When the daily and weekly responsibilities of preparing for, and then preaching and teaching in, the Church and the Great House, were added to the above, it represented a rather heavy work-load.

To the ex-seaman, who had been used to long hours of back-breaking toil, however, this constant round of work for the Lord was no chore.

It was only a pleasure. A privilege, in fact.

For John Newton still hadn't lost his sense of wonder at God's mercy and kindness shown to him. He was always praising Him for his grace. And love. And constant daily care.

To express this sense of gratitude to his Heavenly Father, John Newton wrote many hymns of praise.

In one of these such hymns, he uses very clever repetition of themes and lines to compose an easy-to-remember, and hence sure-to-be-used-at-a-'telling' hymn. It still appears in a number of present-day hymnbooks, but for some reason it never became as popular as many of the others from Olney.

Here then, in full, is John Newton's, 'Praise for Redeeming Love' :-

>Let us love , and sing, and wonder,
>Let us praise the Saviour's name !
>He has hushed the Law's loud thunder,
>He has quenched mount Sinai's flame :
>>He has washed us with his blood,
>>He has brought us nigh to God.

>Let us love the Lord who bought us,
>Pitied us when enemies ;
>Called us by his grace, and taught us,
>Gave us ears, and gave us eyes :
>>He has washed us with his blood,
>>He presents our souls to God.

Orchard Side, the home of William Cowper in the Market Square, Olney, now the Cowper and Newton Museum.

The bridge over the River Ouse. Cowper described the original bridge as being, 'of wearisome but needful length.'

The river meadows where Newton and Cowper often walked and talked together.

The summer house in which the two friends sat chatting for hours on pleasant days.

Cowper's garden at Orchard Side.

Since thou waſt precious in my ſight,
thou haſt been honourable,
Iſaiah. *XLIII*. *4.*th
BUT
Thou ſhalt remember that thou waſt
a bond-man in the land of Egypt,
and the LORD thy God redeemed thee:
Deu.^{my} *XV.* *15.*th

*The inscription above the fireplace in the study at the Vicarage.
The original was in Newton's own handwriting.*

JOHN NEWTON

DIED 21ST DEC^R 1807

AGED 82

MARY NEWTON

DIED 15TH DEC^R 1790

AGED 61.

*John and Mary Newton's tombstone in the grounds of
Olney Parish Church.*

Newton's view of the Church from his study window.

The Vicarage, Olney. Newton's study was on the top storey.

The rear of the Vicarage, with the Church in the background.

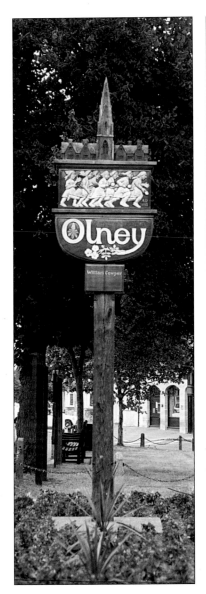 

The town signs in Olney, depicting scenes from its history and including the names of its two famous residents.

The spire of the Parish Church, Olney

"Tall spire, from which the sound of cheerful bells
Just undulates upon the list'ning ear,"

\- The Task, Book 1

Let us sing though fierce temptations
Threaten hard to bear us down !
For the Lord, our strong salvation (u),
Holds in view the conqueror's crown :
    He who washed us with his blood,
    Soon will bring us home to God.

Let us wonder, grace and justice,
Join and point to mercy's store ;
When thro' grace in Christ our trust is,
Justice smiles, and asks no more :
    He who washed us with his blood,
    Has secured our way to God.

Let us praise, and join the chorus
Of the saints, enthroned on high ;
Here they trusted him before us,
Now their praises fill the sky (x) :
    "Thou hast washed us with thy blood,
    Thou art worthy, Lamb of God !"

Hark ! the name of Jesus, sounded
Loud, from golden harps above !
Lord, we blush, and are confounded,
Faint our praises, cold our love !
    Wash our souls and songs with blood,
    For by thee we come to God.

        (u) Revelation 2 v. 10.   (x) Revelation 5 v. 9.
            (Olney Hymns. Book 3. Hymn 82.)

What praise ! What transport ! What utter delight !
What a privilege for the poverty-stricken lacemakers of
Olney to be the first to hear, read from the lips of the great
men themselves, such outpourings of praise !

And who was it, by the way, who said that, "Cowper was a poet, Newton merely a versifier".?!

The regular audiences in the Great House weren't into making such high-brow distinctions. They didn't care a pin. Or a bobbin.

They just loved them both !

And they were led to love God too.

24

'The Clouds Ye So Much Dread'

❖

DURING NOVEMBER AND DECEMBER, 1772, WILLIAM
COWPER BECAME EVEN MORE DEPRESSED. THINGS
WERE CLOSING IN ON HIM. EVERYTHING WAS
BEGINNING TO LOOK BLACK. AND HE COULD SEE
NOT A RAY OF REFRESHING SUNLIGHT.

There were fewer bright days. The 'other days' in his
calendar.

His mind couldn't cope with the pressures.

Discussions had started to take place amongst the women-
folk about the arrangements for his forth-coming wedding to
Mary Unwin in the early part of the next year. He doubted if
he really wanted to go through with that. He was scared of
making such a permanent commitment, and he didn't even
consider himself a worthy partner for Mary. Perhaps he also
felt that he was, in some way or another, betraying his old
friend, and first love, Theadora.

No. Marriage was not for him.

But how could he get out of it without deeply offending dear Mary?

About this time also, Susannah Unwin began to complain to her mother that she considered her care of William Cowper was too much of a drain on her. Especially financially. And urged her to consider making other arrangements.

Susannah's less than total support for her mother's commitment to the constant demands of caring for William Cowper, wasn't exactly a marvellous confidence booster for the nervous poet either.

Then there was John's death. He had never really got over that. Although his brother had gone to be with Christ, he was still gone.

And the agony of his going hadn't been pleasant to watch.

That John Newton had only the best of intentions when he proposed the publication of an Olney hymnbook there can be no doubt. But the constant strain of composing hymns to order almost, was taking its toll too.

It led to a constant process of self-evaluation and assessment.

This, in its turn, led to a sense of self-abasement. Even utter unworthiness.

Cowper had begun to feel like a man in a swamp. Flailing around furiously. Fighting back desperately. But about to go under.

His hymn, 'Temptation', illustrates graphically his anguish of mind and soul. It is a marvellous description of a storm at sea. Cowper's knowledge of things nautical was possibly drawn from his listening to the oft-recounted tales of his ex-captain friend.

The hymn is full of the language of despair. The only hope for the storm-tossed, half-wrecked mariner, is in the appearance of the Saviour. The Pilot.

The author of this poignant hymn needed Divine peace and piloting now, more than ever before :-

> The billows swell, the winds are high,
> Clouds overcast my wintry sky ;
> Out of the depths to thee I call,
> My fears are great, my strength is small.
>
> O LORD, the pilot's part perform,
> And guide and guard me thro' the storm ;
> Defend me from each threatening ill,
> Control the waves, say, "Peace, be still."
>
> Amidst the roaring of the sea,
> My soul still hangs her hope on thee ;
> Thy constant love, thy faithful care,
> Is all that saves me from despair.
>
> Dangers of ev'ry shape and name
> Attend the followers of the Lamb,
> Who leave the world's deceitful shore,
> And leave it to return no more.
>
> Tho' tempest-tossed and half a wreck,
> My Saviour thro' the floods I seek ;
> Let neither winds nor stormy main,
> Force back my shattered bark again.

> (Olney Hymns. Book 3. Hymn 18.)

On New Year's Day, 1773, Cowper went out, alone, for a walk in the fields around Olney.

It was mid-winter. Dull and dark.

As he walked in the chill air the pensive poet had a growing premonition of gathering gloom. The return of mental illness.

On arriving back in Orchard Side, he arranged into an understandable order, and then transcribed into verse, the words and thoughts that had been tumbling around in his mind during the walk.

They represent a sharp contrast.

On one hand he describes the clouds, storms and bitter buds that threatened him. On the other, a resignation to, and reliance upon, the perfection and wisdom of God's power and purpose in the life of the believer.

'Bright designs'. Sweet flowers. And 'a smiling face'.

This was his mental conflict. And he wrote it down. In delicate detail and in an unusual haste, impelled by a sense of the approaching inevitable. But not in the first person singular. It was meant for everybody.

Called, 'Light Shining out of Darkness', it is well-known :-

> God moves in a mysterious way,
>   His wonders to perform ;
> He plants his footsteps in the sea,
>   And rides upon the storm.
>
> Deep in unfathomable mines
>   Of never failing skill ;
> He treasures up his bright designs,
>   And works his sovereign will.
>
> Ye fearful saints fresh courage take,
>   The clouds ye so much dread
> Are big with mercy, and will break
>   In blessings on your head.

Judge not the Lord by feeble sense,
    But trust him for his grace ;
Behind a frowning providence,
    He hides a smiling face.

His purposes will ripen fast,
    Unfolding every hour ;
The bud may have a bitter taste,
    But sweet will be the flower.

Blind unbelief is sure to err (y),
    And scan his work in vain ;
God is his own interpreter,
    And he will make it plain.

(y) John 13 v. 7.
(Olney Hymns. Book 3. Hymn 15.)

Sadly, this was to be the last of the Olney hymns that William Cowper ever wrote.

That night the storm broke.

In all its fury...

25

Trying Times

❖

EARLY NEXT MORNING, 2ND JANUARY, 1773, JOHN NEWTON RECEIVED AN URGENT REQUEST FOR HELP FROM ORCHARD SIDE. WHEN HE HAD HURRIED THROUGH THE GUINEA ORCHARD, HE DISCOVERED THAT HIS WORST FEARS HAD BEEN REALIZED. THE CIRCUMSTANCE THAT HE HAD WORKED SO HARD TO PREVENT, HAD OCCURRED.

William Cowper had again lapsed into insanity.

He was both incoherent and terrified. A heart-rending picture.

Newton was both shocked and stunned. But he determined to stick by his friend. Help him in whatever way he could. They had so much depended upon each other. He couldn't just shrug his shoulders and walk away.

So the busy curate undertook another charge. Oft-every-day visits to the house on the Market Square, to talk to William

Cowper. Try to cheer him up. Bring him through, and out of, his depressed and desolate state of mind.

It was no quick, or easy task.

When he persuaded Cowper to go out for a walk there was a dramatic change from their previous talking-about-anything-and-everything rambles. No lively discussions about politics now. Or literature. Or the Great House. Or the latest hymn.

William Cowper, the brilliant brain, the inspiration for much of their creative work, was reduced to a pathetic imbecility. He had to be guided along, staring blankly into space.

There were occasions when Newton thought, or perhaps tried to convince himself, that his companion's condition was improving.

Late in January he wrote in his diary, "The violence of the storm is, I trust, over."

But he was wrong. It wasn't.

Worse was yet to come.

One night in February, Cowper had a terrible nightmare. In it, he claimed that God spoke to him and said, "Actum est de te, periisti", which being translated means, "It is all over with thee. Thou hast perished".

This 'revelation' shook him to the core. For he believed it. Became convinced that God had cast him off. Rejected him for ever.

John Newton and the two deeply concerned women tried to allay his fears with reassuring words. But to no avail. Sometimes he didn't listen. And on the other occasions when he appeared to be listening, he just didn't seem to understand what they were saying. Or didn't want to understand.

His condition deteriorated further.

Easter Monday was Cattle Fair day in Olney. Farmers and dealers from miles around converged on the market place outside Orchard Side, to buy and sell all sorts of livestock. From early morning until late at night.

The strong language of the 'traders' was usually well lubricated with copious amounts of strong liquor. And the strong odour came free.

William Cowper had always hated that Fair Day. Even at the best of times. It was much too loud. By far too uncouth, for him.

Feeling as he did, on Easter Monday, 12th April 1773, he couldn't bear the thought of it at all. So, as the shouting and lowing, and yelling and neighing, outside the windows began to increase in volume, he and Mary repaired to the Vicarage.

John and Mary made them welcome. Noting the poet's continued agitation, and Mary Unwin's obvious relief at having someone with whom to share the burden, the caring Newtons prepared two separate bedrooms for them. 'So that you can remain overnight, if you wish.'

They did wish. And stayed over that night. And the next one. And the next...

It wasn't long until the astute Newton had the situation summed up. Writing in his diary, he observed, "Now that he is here, he seems desirous to stay".

He was dead right this time !

All through the summer Mary Unwin nursed "Mr. Cowper", as she still insisted in calling him, in the Vicarage. This proved to be a real trial for the patient, motherly figure. Not only had their 'engagement' been long since broken off and forgotten about, but then her difficult charge started to accuse her of trying to get rid of him. By poisoning his food. And she was the only one left whom he trusted to make his meals !

In early October, William Cowper was reckoned to have improved sufficiently to be left in the care of Mary Unwin, while John Newton, accompanied by his wife Mary, set off on a preaching tour.

His condition is described in a letter, dated 7th October, 1773, written from Mary Unwin to the other Mary, when she was away. In it she says :-

> *"Though it will be a sincere pleasure to me to see you &*
> *Dear Mr. Newton again, yet I beg you will not put your-*
> *selves to the least ilconvenience or hurry to reach home*
> *till the most fit & agreeable time. The Lord is very*
> *gracious to us ; for though the cloud of affliction still hangs*
> *heavy on Mr. Cowper yet he is quite calm & persuadable*
> *in every respect. He has been for these few days past*
> *more open & communicative than heretofore..."*

Obviously his condition was not causing her grave concern for she was sufficiently relaxed to ask her friend to do a bit of shopping for her. Bring back a few essentials, and a few luxuries! from Northampton :-

> *"I must beg the favour of you to buy for me two pounds of*
> *Chocolate, half a pound or ten Ounces of white sixpenny*
> *Worsted, half a Dozen Lemons, & two sets of Knitting*
> *Needles, Six in a set, one the finest that can be got of Iron*
> *or Steel, the other a Size Coarser..."*

Despite Mary's impression that Cowper was on the mend, the Newtons did have to hurry home, before their planned visit was over.

William Cowper had again tried to commit suicide.

He came to the conclusion that the only way in which he could regain favour with God, who he still believed had rejected him, was to, "after the example of Abraham, perform an expensive act of obedience, and offer, not a son, but himself".

So he tried to drown himself in the Ouse.

Somehow this attempt was thwarted. God still had other plans for His disturbed child.

The three friends settled into looking after Cowper for the winter in the Vicarage. The constant strain was beginning to tell on all of them. They had each and every one been so patient for so long. So understanding.

John Newton's work pattern began to suffer. He now found hymn-writing very difficult. Almost impossible. How could he possibly write hymns of praise and exultation when his co-writer and constant companion was in such an unsettled state of mind?

It even came to a stage when he found the preparation of his Sunday sermons a problem. To study he resorted to the Great House. There was never prolonged peace and quiet in the Vicarage any more.

Eventually, and blissfully for all concerned, however, the patience of the three concerned carers was rewarded. And their prayers were answered.

During the spring of 1774 Cowper's condition began to improve. Slowly but steadily. He started to show an interest in what was going on around him. And he started to do some things by and for himself, encouraged by those who were by this time unwittingly analysing his every movement. He worked fitfully in the garden, and did some minor repair jobs. And he fed the chickens.

It was when Cowper was feeding the chickens one day in May 1774, that John Newton, who just happened to be watching, caught the faintest, the remotest, glimmer of hope. As he scattered the food from his hand, the chickens were squabbling and squawking, all trying to dive into the same square foot of grain, and Cowper smiled.

For the first time in fourteen months!

Newton soon dashed off to tell the two Marys.

Later in that same month Cowper surprised everybody by announcing that it was about time he and Mrs. Unwin returned to Orchard Side. And when he made that declaration it wasn't long until everybody sprang into action!

In a few more days they were back into the rambling building that had lain almost derelict for over a year.

The move back was a relief. For everybody.

The poet was glad to be back to work in his own house and garden.

Mary Unwin was glad to have him back in his own house and garden. Now she could care for him without the constant conscience of being an imposition on others.

John Newton's diary entry for 28th May, 1774, speaks for itself :-

> *"My dear friends Mrs. Unwin and Mr. Cowper who have been our guests since ye 12 April last year, returned to their home. This is a proof that he is in some respects better, for till very lately he could not bear the proposal of going home. The Lord has graciously interposed in this business... I could not relieve myself, but He has mercifully relieved me".*

Now that a measure of healing and relief had come everything could move on again.

But not, as it turned out, with the same level of spiritual commitment by Cowper to the hymn-writing enterprise.

That had gone forever.

26

Puss And Tiny, Bess And Betsy

❖

WITH THE RETURN OF WILLIAM AND MARY TO
ORCHARD SIDE, THE BUSINESS OF DAILY LIVING
TOOK ON A NEW AND BRIGHTER DIMENSION FOR
EVERYBODY.

Cowper's condition continued to improve steadily.
Although he wrote very little for a while, he became involved
in other, more practical, interests.

The first of these interests was developed in a remarkable
way.

One day a lad from the town had been roaming in the fields
and found an abandoned leveret. He brought it home. His
parents, either not wanting the tiny creature, or not knowing
what to do with it, encouraged him to show it to Sir Cowper,
who had always been advocating kindness to animals.

On seeing the poor, pathetic little thing, William Cowper
offered to attempt to raise it. He would at least give it a home.

It wasn't long until the news spread around Olney, "Sir Cowper knows how to look after baby hares!"

And it wasn't long after that until he was offered more. It became a regular occurrence for groups of children, excitedly chattering about the latest leveret they had found, to turn up on the doorstep of Orchard Side. To offer it to the strange-and-quiet but nonetheless warm-and-friendly man who lived there.

He eventually ended up caring for three baby hares, calling them Puss, Tiny and Bess. They were, he told anyone took any notice of them, "all males, despite the two feminine appellatives."

The care of these baby animals, which Cowper first undertook in the summer of 1774, proved to be excellent therapy. He immediately started to tame them, make cages for them, and find out about their diet. It was involvement outside of himself. His endeavours with the hares must have been successful, too, for he kept them as pets for years.

Another hobby in which William Cowper renewed his interest upon his return to Orchard Side was gardening. He had always been a fairly keen gardener, but now there was a lot of work to be done. After fourteen months of virtual neglect the whole garden had become unkempt and overgrown. It was a mess.

The creative mind of the poet didn't stop at pulling weeds and tidying borders, however. He was an innovative gardener. Always experimenting with new plants and seeds. Mary Newton, who spent any spare time she had working in the vicarage garden, was a tremendous encouragement to him in this respect. Talking to him about his newest enterprises and even bringing him seeds and plants from London when she could.

This preoccupation with gardening also helped William Cowper to employ his D.I. Y. abilities to good effect. He built a frame and also a heated greenhouse in which he grew melons, cucumbers and even pineapples. Although he didn't seem to eat much of his own produce himself, he took great delight in giving it away to his friends. Providing them with fresh pineapples in January was to prove one of the pleasures of his later life.

One of Cowper's most useful garden constructions was the quaint summer-house which he erected at the top end of the garden, on the path from the Guinea Orchard. There he sat for hours on good days, planning his next project, or just surveying the flowering plants around him.

A frequent visitor to the summer-house was John Newton, who kept a watchful and caring eye on his friend. They sat through summer-scented afternoons, chatting away.

Newton wanted to encourage the becoming-more-reasonable Cowper back along the spiritual paths which he had once travelled with such delight, and to hear what he had to say about anything and everything. To be there for him.

And he wanted to tell him about the latest addition to their household. Betsy.

Betsy Catlett was Mary Newton's niece. Her mother had died at her birth, and her father, George Catlett, died five years later, leaving little Betsy an orphan. Mary, who had cared for her sick brother during his final illness, had become very fond of the lively Betsy, and she and John at once volunteered to adopt the child.

Initially, Mary's father, and Betsy's grandfather, old George Catlett, who was both a widower and an invalid, and therefore unable to care for the child himself, expressed concern about this proposition. He reckoned that the couple who were approaching their silver wedding anniversary would find it difficult to cope with a frisky five-year-old. Perhaps John Newton, the busy curate, would have neither the time or the inclination to take on Mary's niece as his own, either.

Grandfather needn't have worried, however. The arrangement went ahead, for there were just no other options. The child had to be cared for by somebody, somewhere. And the adoption of Betsy in the late summer of 1774 turned out to be one of the best things ever to happen in the married life of John and Mary Newton.

The vicarage at Olney reverberated with childish shouts and laughter for the first time in at least ten years, and her adoptive parents seemed to shed years off their lives. They approached everything with a new sense of vigour. They had to. They had no choice in the matter really, for Betsy was so vigorous. So alert. So full of life.

Great for them all.

A whole new stage in their lives was unfolding. A new vista was opening up before them.

William Cowper, was happily reinstated in Orchard Side with the ever-patient, caring Mary, his garden, and his pets. Three hares, two dogs, a number of cats, and birds and fish of various sorts and sizes.

John and Mary Newton now had Betsy.

So with his ailing companion apparently well on the road to mental health and stability, and Betsy buzzing around to inject new zest into everything, John Newton recovered his 'harp' from 'the willows' where he had 'hung' it, about eighteen months earlier. And pressed his pen back into service, as well.

He returned to work, in earnest, for there was a lot of catching up to be done.

Writing hymns for the Great House.

On his own, this time.

27

Just Don't Be Afraid To Ask

--- ❖ ---

LIKE MANY SPIRITUAL TEACHERS, OF WHATEVER DENOMINATION, JOHN NEWTON HAD FAVOURITE THEMES. AND TEXTS.

Since most of his hymns were written to be expounded at prayer meetings in the Great House, and because he had experienced some remarkable answers to prayer in his lifetime, not least of which was the steady recovery of his friend, William Cowper, a recurring theme in his hymns was prayer. The privilege of approaching 'the throne of grace'. Of 'coming to a King'. And asking for all that we need.

There was also a Bible passage from which he often read, and which he used as a starting-point from which to teach on the subject. It was God's word to Solomon in 1 Kings chapter 3.

"Ask what I shall give thee," He said. (verse 5).

Newton must have resorted to this story and text in his preaching more than once, for he wrote no less than three hymns based upon it.

One of the three called, 'If Solomon for wisdom prayed,' could hardly be described as ranking amongst Newton's best work, but the other two were both sufficiently noteworthy both in style and content, for selected verses from them to be still around today.

Here they are, in full, as they came from the pen of Newton. As the congregation in the Great House heard them on prayer-meeting night.

The first is called, 'The Throne of Grace.' :-

> Behold the throne of grace !
> The promise calls me near ;
> There Jesus shows a smiling face,
> And waits to answer prayer.
>
> That rich atoning blood,
> Which sprinkled round I see ;
> Provides for those who come to God,
> An all-prevailing plea.
>
> My soul ask what thou wilt,
> Thou canst not be too bold ;
> Since his own blood for thee he spilt,
> What else can he withhold.
>
> Beyond thy utmost wants
> His love and power can bless ;
> To praying souls he always grants,
> More than they can express.

Since 'tis the Lord's command,
My mouth I open wide ;
Lord open thou thy bounteous hand,
That I may be supplied.

Thine image, Lord, bestow,
Thy presence and thy love ;
I ask to serve thee here below,
And reign with thee above.

Teach me to live by faith,
Conform my will to thine ;
Let me victorious be in death,
And then in glory shine.

If Thou these blessings give,
And wilt my portion be ;
Cheerful the world's poor toys I leave,
To them who know not thee.

(Olney Hymns. Book 1. Hymn 33.)

The other significant hymn of Newton's on the same text, has a similar theme throughout. The wonder of redemption to God through the blood of Christ, and the access thus afforded to Christians to the throne of grace. To bring 'large petitions'.

Its title, 'Come my Soul, thy Suit Prepare,' could prove confusing for some. This has nothing whatsoever to do with getting your best clothes ironed in time for the Sunday Morning Service in church. The 'suit' of the hymn is the request or petition which we are exhorted to have ready when coming to God in prayer.

So great is our God that no request can ever be beyond the bounds of His power to grant.

It is noticeable that John Newton's initial request was for the removal of 'this load of sin !' How conscious he was of his propensity to sin. Still. Even as an active curate in a busy parish.

The hymn, then. As it first appeared :-

Come my soul, thy suit prepare,
Jesus loves to answer prayer ;
He himself has bid thee pray,
Therefore will not say thee nay.

Thou art coming to a King (r),
Large petitions with thee bring ;
For his grace and power are such,
None can ever ask too much.

With my burden I begin,
Lord, remove this load of sin !
Let thy blood, for sinners spilt,
Set my conscience free from guilt.

Lord ! I come to thee for rest,
Take possession of my breast ;
There thy blood-bought right maintain,
And without a rival reign.

As the image in the glass
Answers the beholder's face ;
Thus unto my heart appear,
Print thine own resemblance there.

While I am a pilgrim here,
Let thy love my spirit cheer ;
As my Guide, my Guard, my Friend,
Lead me to my journey's end.

Show me what I have to do,
Ev'ry hour my strength renew ;
Let me live a life of faith,
Let me die thy people's death.

(r) Psalm 81 v.10.
(Olney Hymns. Book 1. Hymn 31.)

Another topic that appears time and time again in John Newton's hymns, displaying the extent of his knowledge of the Scriptures, occurs in the sixth verse of, 'Come my Soul, thy Suit Prepare'.

'My Guide, my Guard, my Friend...'

It is the names and titles given to our Saviour, the Lord Jesus Christ.

Newton uses such a wide variety of them, and with such effect. Yet there is a warmth, almost an intimacy, of feeling about the use of the titles that would lead us to conclude that he had met and communed with the Lord, had practical experience of Him, in all His different roles and positions. They are more than mere words.

One of these hymns has become justly famous.

One stands out above all others...

28

Dear Name!

---------------- ❖ ----------------

ONE DAY, AS JOHN NEWTON WAS PREPARING HIS
SERMON FOR CHURCH ON THE FOLLOWING
SUNDAY, OR FOR THE GREAT HOUSE PRAYER-
MEETING IN THE MIDDLE OF THE WEEK, HE WAS
REFLECTING UPON SONG OF SOLOMON CH.1, V.3.
"THY NAME IS AS OINTMENT POURED FORTH."

He allowed his mind to drift back to his wild and rebellious past. The only times that he had ever used the name of
Jesus then had been as an oath. In blasphmeny. As vehement
and vitriolic as he could make it.

Then he considered the change. It had all started that day
on the deck of the 'Greyhound', when he had breathed the
name of the Lord in a last-ditch prayer.

From that time onward the name of Jesus had begun to
mean something different to him. And as the days and years
had advanced, he began to appreciate just how much.

On the 'Greyhound', Jesus Christ had become John Newton's Saviour.

When he started to delve deeply into the Word of God, however, and live the Christian life in a godless world, he discovered that not only was Jesus a wonderful Saviour to him. He was a lot of other things besides.

His Lord was the ever-present source of inner healing, spiritual food, dependable shelter, and daily provision.

So he started to express these sentiments in verse.

The quill moved painfully slowly across the paper, for the writer paused frequently, searching for the dead-right word or phrase...

It was hard. Explaining what the Saviour meant to him in rhyming words. Language was so restrictive.

Eventually there lay on his desk a lovely hymn. One which the congregation at Olney may not have appreciated above any of the others, for their curate was now busily producing a hymn a week, but one which has since been sung with deep feeling by millions of people around the world. The one that occurs in more Christian hymnbooks, perhaps, than any other of John Newton's hymns.

It has universal appeal.

Here it is. 'The Name of JESUS' :-

> How sweet the name of JESUS sounds,
>   In a believer's ear ?
> It soothes his sorrows, heals his wounds,
>   And drives away his fear.
>
> It makes the wounded spirit whole,
>   And calms the troubled breast ;
> 'Tis Manna to the hungry soul,
>   And to the weary rest.

Dear name ! the rock on which I build,
   My shield and hiding place ;
My never-failing treasury filled
   With boundless stores of grace.

By thee my prayers acceptance gain,
   Although with sin defiled ;
Satan accuses me in vain,
   And I am owned a child.

JESUS ! my Shepherd, Husband, Friend,
   My Prophet, Priest, and King ;
My Lord, my Life, my Way, my End,
   Accept the praise I bring.

Weak is the effort of my heart,
   And cold my warmest thought ;
But when I see thee as thou art,
   I'll praise thee as I ought.

'Till then I would thy love proclaim
   With every fleeting breath ;
And may the music of thy name
   Refresh my soul in death.

(Olney Hymns. Book1. Hymn 57.)

All those who are familiar with this hymn, who have been
both encouraged and challenged while singing it at some stage
in their lifetime, will quickly notice that our modern
hymnbooks all contain two substantial changes to Newton's
original. An omission. And an alteration.

Most, if not all, omit the fourth verse. It was considered,
possibly with some justification, by those who compiled our

hymnbooks, to break the flow of the hymn. To be so far removed from its central theme, the name of Jesus, to be best omitted.

The alteration is to the first line of verse five. The concept of Jesus as Husband proved unacceptable to most. It was regarded as either doctrinally dubious or just too familiar, or both. So most hymnbooks change it, substituting either 'Saviour' or 'Brother', for 'Husband'.

Despite these minor modifications, 'How sweet the name of Jesus sounds', has endured to become a best-loved hymn of the Christian church for more than two centuries.

It contains Newton's frank confession of personal inadequacy when contemplating the work and worth of the Saviour. True believers, for over two hundred years, have identified with him in this, admitting,

> "Weak is the effort of my heart,
>
> And cold my warmest thought..."

Two of John Newton's most frequently used Scriptural titles of Christ also appear in this hymn. Titles which even a casual reading of all his hymns will reveal.

Cropping up, time and time again.

They are worth looking into...

29

My Friend, The Shepherd

❖

DURING HIS LIFETIME, JOHN NEWTON MADE MANY FRIENDS.

Some of them, though, deserted him at his conversion, totally unable to understand his sudden interest in 'religion'. Others of his Christian friends were very dear to him. In some cases, though, the warmth from the fire of their friendship, with the passage of time, was also reduced to smouldering embers. For instance, what had once been a sharing communion between himself and Martin Madan ended rather unpleasantly. They disagreed about doctrine.

In other cases, his friends let him down. They were just not able to live up to his expectations of them. Couldn't deliver. It was a sad blow to him, for example, when his close companion, William Cowper, wasn't able, because of his illness, to continue with the writing of hymns for their proposed joint venture. An Olney hymnbook.

So the belief in Jesus as his Friend became both an inspiration and a consolation to him. Hadn't He said, when speaking to His disciples just a day or two before His death, "Ye are my friends, if ye do whatsoever I command you."? (John 15 v.14).

Although the title of Friend occurs in a number of his hymns, on one occasion Newton, using as a sermon text Absalom's question to Hushai in 2 Samuel 16, "Is this thy kindness to thy friend ?"(v.17), wrote a specific hymn on the subject.

The hymn runs to eight verses, but it would appear that only the first three were ever used in Christian hymnbooks. Those who compiled the hymnals may have reckoned that the remaining verses, where Newton berates himself for his inability to reciprocate the Saviour's friendship, are too self-abasing. Too personal. Or perhaps too painfully precise !

The first three verses are, there can be no doubt, encouraging. Uplifting. Reassuring. But what of the rest?

Was John Newton the only one who ever felt like this ? :-

> Poor, weak, and worthless tho' I am,
> I have a rich almighty friend ;
> JESUS, the Saviour, is his name,
> He freely loves, and without end.

> He ransomed me from hell with blood,
> And by his power my foes controlled ;
> He found me, wandering far from God,
> And brought me to his chosen fold.

> He cheers my heart, my want supplies,
> And says that I shall shortly be
> Enthroned with him above the skies,
> Oh ! what a friend is Christ to me.

But ah ! my inmost spirit mourns,
And well my eyes with tears may swim,
To think of my perverse returns ;
I've been a faithless friend to him.

Often my gracious Friend I grieve,
Neglect, distrust, and disobey,
And often Satan's lies believe,
Sooner than all my Friend can say.

He bids me always freely come,
And promises whate'er I ask :
But I am straitened, cold and dumb,
And count my privilege a task.

Before the world that hates his course,
My treacherous heart has throbbed with shame ;
Loth to forego the world's applause,
I hardly dare avow his name.

Sure were not I most vile and base,
I could not thus my friend requite !
And were not he the God of grace,
He'd frown and spurn me from his sight.

(Olney Hymns. Book 1. Hymn 30)

The second title of the Lord Jesus that is frequently used by John Newton in his writings, is that of Shepherd.

Often as he travelled the roads around Olney, either walking with his friend William Cowper, or riding on horse-back on his way to visit the sick or conduct a service in some remote rural location, he would have noticed the sheep grazing peacefully in the meadows. Such pastoral scenes were, to him, constant reminders of the promise of Psalm 23 v.1, "The Lord is my shepherd ; I shall not want."

His understanding of the extended metaphor of God's people as sheep, with Jesus as their caring Shepherd, is fully displayed in a hymn which he wrote expanding the theme for his congregation. He called it simply, 'Sheep'.

He must have appreciated the nature of some other animals in addition to his 'sheep', as verse two would indicate. Perhaps he had heard plenty about hares from his by-now-recovering companion !

Some literary critics may have difficulty in describing the verses that follow as poetry, but some anxious Christians would have no difficulty whatsoever in obtaining strength and solace from the comforting thoughts they express :-

> The Saviour calls his people sheep,
> And bids them on his love rely ;
> For he alone their souls can keep,
> And he alone their wants supply.
>
> The bull can fight, the hare can flee,
> The ant, in summer food prepare ;
> But helpless sheep, and such are we,
> Depend upon the Shepherd's care.
>
> JEHOVAH is our Shepherd's name (z),
> Then what have we, though weak, to fear ?
> Our sin and folly we proclaim,
> If we despair while he is near.
>
> When Satan threatens to devour,
> When troubles press on every side ;
> Think of our Shepherd's care and power,
> He can defend, he will provide.

See the rich pastures of his grace,
Where, in full streams, salvation flows !
There he appoints our resting place,
And we may feed, secure from foes.

There 'midst the flock the Shepherd dwells,
The sheep around in safety lie ;
The wolf, in vain, with malice swells,
For he protects them with his eye (a).

Dear Lord, if I am one of thine,
From anxious thoughts I would be free ;
To trust, and love, and praise, is mine,
The care of all belongs to thee.

(z) Psalm 23 v.1   (a) Micah 5 v. 4
(Olney Hymns. Book 2. Hymn 94.)

As he approached the age of fifty John Newton began to come to terms with the fact that he was not just as fit and well as he used to be.

Writing in his diary, early in 1774, he observed, "I begin to feel the effects of the advancing years and gentle intimations that the health and strength I have long been favoured with, will not always last."

He was right. His health was declining.

In the autumn of 1776, John Newton had to be admitted to Guy's Hospital, London, to have operation to remove a tumour from his thigh.

The prospect of this forthcoming operation and his forced absence from his parishioners in Olney must have weighed heavily on his active mind. For he wrote a hymn, which he introduced to his congregations, before he left them for the capital.

It is moving to note the extent of his very natural concern
about the future, as expressed in the latter half of verse six :-

'Give us, if we live, ere long
Here to meet in peace again.'

Whatever lay ahead, however, John Newton was able to
commit himself into the loving care of his 'tender Shepherd',
and confidently rely on his 'ever-present Friend'.

And there they are again ! Favourite titles. Comforting con-
cepts.

Many hearts would have been touched as John Newton
taught his audiences this hymn, just before he set off for London with Mary :-

At Parting.

As the sun's enlivening eye
Shines on every place the same ;
So the Lord is always nigh
To the souls that love his name.

When they move at duty's call,
He is with them by the way ;
He is ever with them all,
Those who go, and those who stay.

From his holy mercy-seat
Nothing can their souls confine ;
Still in spirit they may meet,
And in sweet communion join.

For a season called to part,
Let us then ourselves commend
To the gracious eye and heart,
Of our ever-present Friend.

Jesus, hear our humble prayer !
Tender Shepherd of thy sheep !
Let thy mercy and thy care
All our souls in safety keep.

In thy strength may we be strong,
Sweeten every cross and pain ;
Give us, if we live, ere long
Here in peace to meet again.

Then, if thou thy help afford,
Ebenezers shall be reared ;
And our souls shall praise the Lord
Who our poor petitions heard.

(Olney Hymns. Book 2. Hymn 71.)

Thankfully for all concerned their parting was not for good. Not yet.

Newton's Friend, the Shepherd, strengthened him during his operation, sweetened his pain during recovery, and returned him to meet with the people of Olney again in November.

Mary Unwin and William Cowper were glad to see him back. They had been worried about him. And had been praying for him.

And most of the townsfolk were glad to see him back too. Most. But not all...

30

'Tell It Not In Gath!'

❖

JOHN NEWTON WAS OUT OF OLNEY, PROBABLY
ENGAGED IN ONE OF THE MANY ASPECTS OF
CHURCH BUSINESS, WHEN A SERIOUS FIRE BROKE
OUT IN THE TOWN, ON 22ND SEPTEMBER, 1777. A
THATCHED COTTAGE HAD CAUGHT FIRE, AND
BEFORE THE TOWNSPEOPLE COULD EXTINGUISH
THE BLAZE WITH THEIR BUCKETS OF WATER, EIGHT
COTTAGES HAD BEEN TOTALLY DESTROYED AND
OTHERS EXTENSIVELY DAMAGED. ONLY A GAP
BETWEEN THE DWELLINGS AND A CHANGE IN THE
DIRECTION OF THE WIND HAD SAVED THE TOWN
FROM DEVASTATION.

When the curate of the parish returned from his trip and
witnessed the destruction caused by the fire, he immediately
set up a relief fund. It wasn't long until a number of his wealthy
London contacts had contributed four hundred and fifty

pounds for the rebuilding of the burnt-out homes. This relief was extremely welcome because the meagre livelihood of the pillow lace makers was now under threat from machine-made lace in the cities.

The already-poor were only set to become poorer.

And they had never heard of insurance.

However, Newton, believing that prevention where possible, is better than cure, recognised that another flashpoint, literally, was approaching. Guy Fawkes Night on the 5th of November.

He expressed his concern about the fire risk involved in lighted candles in every window and flaming torches, usually brandished by drunken youths, in the streets. The town's celebration committee, appreciating the sound sense of his observations, asked him to make an announcement in church.

Understanding this decision to have 'wide acceptance in the town', John Newton set about approaching the matter with his usual thoroughness.

During the evening service on Sunday 2nd November he spoke against the excesses of drunken revelry, and advocated caution on the coming Wednesday night.

In the course of his sermon, to emphasise the potentially serious nature of the situation he introduced a hymn, recalling that frantic and frightening night, back in September.

He hoped to get the idea across. Graphically. In easy-to-remember verse :-

On The Fire at Olney. September 22, 1777.

> Wearied by day with toils and cares,
> How welcome is the peaceful night !
> Sweet sleep our wasted strength repairs,
> And fits us for returning light.

Yet when our eyes in sleep are closed,
Our rest may break ere well begun ;
To dangers ev'ry hour exposed
We neither can forsee or shun.

'Tis of the Lord that we can sleep
A single night without alarms ;
His eye alone our lives can keep
Secure , amidst a thousand harms.

For months and years of safety past,
Ungrateful, we, alas! have been ;
Though patient long, he spoke at last,
And bid the fire rebuke our sin.

The shout of "Fire!", a dreadful cry,
Impressed each heart with deep dismay ;
While the fierce blaze and red'ning sky,
Made midnight wear the face of day.

The throng and terror who can speak?
The various sounds that filled the air !
The infant's wail, the mother's shriek,
The voice of blasphemy and prayer !

But prayer prevailed, and saved the town ;
The few, who loved the Saviour's name,
Were heard, and mercy hasted down
To change the wind, and stop the flame.

Oh, may that night be ne'er forgot !
Lord, still increase thy praying few !
Were Olney left without a Lot,
Ruin, like Sodoms', would ensue.

(Olney Hymns. Book 2. Hymn 69.)

Unfortunately, the admonition, however well-intentioned, was not altogether gratefully received by a number of the rebellious would-be revellers in the town.

They determined that they wouldn't tolerate any interfering minister telling them how to conduct their celebrations. They would do it just as they liked. And possibly, just for badness, carry it to even greater lengths than before.

The evening's 'festivities' began when a mob, armed with cudgels, paraded the town smashing every window that didn't have a candle in it.

Newton's diary entry for 5th November, 1777, indicates that he was aware that the opposition of the rioters had been intensified by his intervention in the matter. He wrote;-

> *"An attempt to restrain the licentiousness that has usually prevailed on the return of this day, and to lessen the probability of Fire raised such a spirit of opposition and defiance as I never saw before. The streets were paraded in the evening by the Sons of Belial who filled the town with violence and terror."*

Later on in the evening the parading mob decided to vent its fury on John Newton. And his home. The vicarage.

About ten o'clock a breathless friend knocked furiously at the door, yelling to the Newtons that the mob was heading in that direction, 'swearing to break every window in the place.'

A letter which John Newton wrote to the generous merchant, Thornton, a few days later, describes what happened then :-

> *'... upon a friend's bringing word about ten in the evening, that forty or fifty of them, full of fury and liquor, were just coming to beset us, Mrs. Newton was so terrified,*

and her head so much affected, as it always is upon any
alarm, that I was forced to send an embassage and beg
peace. A soft message, and a shilling to the captain of the
mob, secured his protection and we slept in safety. Alas,
'tell it not in Gath!' I am ashamed of the story.'

Obviously the ex-sea captain who had dealt successfully
with both mutinous crews and escaping slaves, regretted not
having the opportunity to deal with the mob as he would have
liked. To single out the ring-leader and reason with him.

And he regretted something else as well. Something much
more insidious. Much more difficult to deal with.

An entry in his diary, a few days later, complains of "such
inconsistencies as cross, passionate, bigotted and selfish
Christians", and asks the question, "are not these things as
contrary to Thy spirit as drunkenness and theft?"

The riot in Olney on Guy Fawkes night, 1777, just served
to press home to the mind of the perceptive churchman something which he had come to realize, rather painfully.

Opposition to him, and the style and content of his preaching, was growing in the town.

The first rumblings of a 'Newton must go!' campaign had
begun.

31

A Lion In Olney

---❖---

MEANWHILE, WILLIAM COWPER'S CONDITION WAS
IMPROVING STEADILY. HIS INTEREST IN GARDEN-
ING AND THE CARE OF HIS MANY PETS KEPT HIS
MIND OFF WEIGHTIER MATTERS. HE STARTED TO
WALK IN THE COUNTRY AGAIN AND HE AND JOHN
NEWTON CONVERSED REGULARLY. IN THE SUMMER
HOUSE ON PLEASANT DAYS. IN THE PARLOUR OF
EITHER HOUSE ON WET ONES.

It was a sign of his stabilizing state of mind that he started
writing again. Not only did he compose some poetry for his
own amusement, but he also wrote many letters. William
Cowper was a consistent and witty correspondent.

In one of his letters to William Unwin, he described, with
wry humour, the visit of a caged lion as an attraction to the
Cherry Fair in Olney in late June, 1778. This fair was an
altogether more light-hearted affair than the Easter Monday

cattle fair. It was more like a carnival than a trading fair, and Cowper, with his keen eye and quick wit, relished the opportunity to have a look at life around him.

In the letter, dated Saturday 18th July, 1778, he writes :-

"...a Lion was imported here at the Fair, Seventy Years of Age, & as tame as a   Goose. Your Mother and I saw him embrace his Keeper with his Paws, and lick his Face. Others saw him receive his Head in his Mouth, and restore it to him   again unhurt. A Sight we chose not to be favoured with, but rather advised the Honest Man to discontinue the Practice. A Practice hardly reconcileable to Prudence, unless he had a Head to spare. The Beast however was a very Magnificent one, and much more Royal in his Appearance, than those I have seen in the Tower..."

John Newton must also have spent some time in the Cherry Fair that day. And he must also have seen the lion. Such was his God-centred, self-abasing, spiritual condition, however, that he learnt something entirely different from it than the poet. He saw himself reflected in its nature.

He also mentioned it to a colleague in a letter. Writing to William Bull, Congregational minister in Newport Pagnell, and a friend of both himself and Cowper, on June 30th, he observed :-

"Last week we had a lion in the town. I went to see him. He was wonderfully tame, as familiar with his keeper and as docile and obedient as a spaniel, yet the man told me that he had surly fits, when they dare not touch him. No looking-glass could express my face more justly than this lion did my heart. I could trace every feature. As wild and fierce by nature, yea, much more so, but grace has in some measure tamed me. I know and love my Keeper, and some-

*times watch His looks, that I might learn His will. But
oh! I have my surly fits too. Seasons when I relapse into
the savage again, as though I had forgotten all. I got a
hymn out of this lion, which you shall see when you come
to Olney, if you please me."*

The hymn about the lion would certainly have been topical when Newton introduced it to his congregation:-

The Tamed Lion

A Lion, tho' by nature wild
　　The art of man can tame ;
He stands before his keeper, mild,
　　And gentle as a lamb.

He watches, with submissive eye,
　　The hand that gives him food ;
As if he meant to testify
　　A sense of gratitude.

But man himself, who thus subdues
　　The fiercest beasts of prey ;
A nature, more unfeeling shows,
　　And far more fierce than they.

Tho' by the Lord preserved and fed,
　　He proves rebellious still ;
And while he eats his Maker's bread,
　　Resists his holy will.

Alike in vain, of grace that saves,
　　Or threat'ning law he hears ;
The savage scorns, blasphemes, and raves,
　　But neither loves nor fears.

O Saviour ! how thy wondrous power
By angels is proclaimed !
When in thine own appointed hour,
They see the lion tamed.

The love thy bleeding cross displays,
The hardest heart subdues ;
Here furious lions while they gaze,
Their rage and fierceness lose (y).

Yet we are but renewed in part,
The lion still remains ;
Lord, drive him wholly from my heart,
Or keep him fast in chains.

(y) Isaiah 11 v.6
(Olney Hymns. Book2. Hymn 93.)

Towards the end of that year, 1778, John Newton became
increasingly concerned that his days of useful service in Olney
were coming to an end. The roaring of the untamed lion, and
a few growls from the tamed one too, sounded timely warn-
ings.

Although he had worked tirelessly for all his parishioners,
he was criticised by many of the landed gentry for being far
too friendly with the common and ignorant people. Too
worried about their everyday needs, and too ready to encourage them to participate in prayer in the Great House.

The hierarchy of the established church had a problem with
him as well. For them he associated too much with the
Dissenters, even permitting William Bull and other Baptist
ministers to share in his services from time to time.

This didn't go down too well either.

Then there was the increasing, and up until that time, uncharacteristic, apathy amongst his own congregation. This worried him most. Far more than outright antagonism. As a sea-captain he had come to expect rebellion and opposition and had learnt to cope with them. But a loss of confidence and support from those for whom he had laboured and prayed so hard, was something else. A bitter pill to swallow.

Once, during his opening remarks, in a prayer meeting at the Great House, he decided to 'test the water'. And he advanced the idea of possibly seeking a move to another parish. His diary entry for that evening draws its own conclusions from the response of the congregation. He wrote, "I could not but notice that they who prayed after I had done speaking, though they prayed affectionately for me, did not put up one direct petition for my continuance."

Another diary entry, late in 1778, makes the sad observation, "Things seem to decline around me. The Great House is thin...and the church very thin."

Perhaps God was trying to tell him something.

Perhaps it was time to move on. But there was one thing, one big thing, that he had to see finished before he left. It was well advanced, and he couldn't abandon it now...

32

For Public Worship, By Plain People

❖

FOR ALMOST TEN YEARS JOHN NEWTON HAD BEEN COLLECTING AND CATALOGUING ALL THE HYMNS THAT HE AND HIS FRIEND WILLIAM COWPER HAD WRITTEN, AND NOW HE BELIEVED THAT THE TIME HAD COME TO PUT HIS PLAN FOR THEM INTO ACTION.

Before he did anything else, or went anywhere else, he had an ambition to fulfil. And a long standing agreement with a friend to honour.

It was time to publish. To go into print.

Just one matter worried him a bit though. Not the material. He had plenty of that. Copies of hymns were crammed into drawers and chests all over the vicarage. And he was convinced that they were all good. People would probably like most of them.

No. His problem was not with the material. It was with the money. Publishing could be a costly business. He needed someone to back the project financially. A sponsor.

Here again the wealthy and benevolent John Thornton came to the rescue.

He undertook to buy and distribute one thousand copies. Newton reckoned that he himself had sufficient contacts to dispose of a further thousand, but he promised to plough any profits back into the venture. In a letter which he wrote to John Thornton on the matter, he stated his qualms of conscience thus, "...should there be any profit I would like to throw it into the common Stock, thereby lessening the burden which you are pleased to bear in my concerns. For I believe my mind would not be quite easy, if I was to hoard up anything that might arise from the sale of spiritual things..."

So, early in 1779, he decided to publish. First print run, two thousand.

Having amassed all the hymns for the collection, and arranged them into an acceptable order, John Newton sat down to write the preface to the volume, which was to be called simply, 'Olney Hymns, in Three Books.'

This preface is an extremely well-expressed explanation of the purpose and content of the volume, falling as it does into four distinct sections. Though Newton may not have planned it that precisely, it is evident that his intention was to clarify three different aspects of the collection. The purpose for which it was written, the style in which it was written, and the actual format of the hymnbook itself. All this, crowned by an ungrudging dedication, make sizeable portions of it worth recording.

The opening paragraphs of the preface advance three reasons why the hymnbook was even considered necessary, in the first place. For the proclamation of the Christian faith, the perpetuation of a valued friendship, and the establishment of the authorship of some of the hymns, which had already begun to appear elsewhere, attributed wrongly to other authors.

As though setting out to convince a somewhat doubtful readership, Newton states his case with both clarity and conviction :-

"Copies of a few of these hymns have already appeared in periodical publications, and in some recent collections. I have observed one or two of them attributed to persons who certainly had no concern in them, but as transcribers...The public may be assured that the whole number were composed by two persons only.The original design would not admit of any other association. A desire of promoting the faith and comfort of sincere Christians, though the principal, was not the only motive to this undertaking. It was likewise intended as a monument, to perpetuate the remembrance of an intimate and endeared friendship. With this pleasing view I entered upon my part, which would have been smaller than it is, and the book would have appeared much sooner, and in a very different form, if the wise, though mysterious providence of God, had not seen fit to cross my wishes. We had not proceeded far upon the proposed plan, before my friend was prevented, by a long and affecting indisposition, from affording me any farther assistance. My grief and disappointment were great ; I hung my harp on the willows, and for some time thought myself determined to proceed no farther without him. Yet my mind was afterwards led to resume the service. My progress in it, amidst a variety of other engagements, has been slow, yet in the course of years the hymns amounted to a considerable number : And

my deference to the judgment and desires of others, has at length overcome the reluctance I long felt to see them in print, while I had so few of my friend's hymns to insert in the collection. Though it is possible a good judge of composition might be able to distinguish those which are his, I have thought it proper to preclude a misapplication, by prefixing the letter C to each of them. For the rest I must be responsible."

When dealing with the style in which the hymns were written, Newton was careful to stress that an unmistakable presentation of Scriptural truth was the chief object for which they were written. Embellishments of purely poetical, but spiritually shallow, language, were to be avoided :-

"There is a stile and manner suited to the composition of hymns, which may be more successfully, or at least more easily attained by a versifier, than a poet. They should be hymns, not odes, if designed for public worship, and for the use of plain people. Perspicuity, simplicity and ease, should chiefly be attended to ; and the imagery and colouring of poetry, if admitted at all, should be indulged very sparingly and with great judgment. The late Dr. Watts, many of whose hymns are admirable patterns in this species of writing, might, as a poet, have a right to say, That it cost him some labour to restrain his fire and to accommodate himself to the capacities of common readers. But it would not become me to make such a declaration. It behoved me to do my best. But though I would not offend readers of taste by a wilful coarseness, and negligence, I do not write professedly for them. If the Lord whom I serve, has been pleased to favour me with that mediocrity of talent, which may qualify me for usefulness

to the weak and poor of his flock, without quite disgust-
ing persons of superior discernment, I have reason to be
satisfied."

Like Dr. Watts before him, and many of his successors, John
Newton decided to classify his hymns under separate head-
ings. 'Three books', he called his divisions. So for the conven-
ience of all those who would choose to use the hymnbook,
the preface included this practical explanation of its layout :-

"The Hymns are distributed into three Books. In the first
I have classed those which are formed upon select
passages of Scripture, and placed them in the order of the
books of the Old and New Testament. The second
contains occasional Hymns, suited to particular seasons,
or suggested by particular events or objects.The third book
is miscellaneous, comprising a variety of subjects relative
to a life of faith in the Son of God, which have no express
reference either to a single text of Scripture, or to any
determinate season or incident."

The final section of the preface to the hymnbook is a touching dedication to Christians everywhere, and of all ages, but
more especially to the townsfolk of Olney. The very people,
many of whom had long since lost the appetite for their
curate's hymn-written expositions at the Great House. And
wouldn't even be too upset if he decided to move on to somewhere else :-

"This publication, which, with my humble prayer to the
Lord for his blessing upon it, I offer to the service of all
those who love the Lord Jesus Christ in sincerity, of every
name and in every place, into whose hands it may come ;

I more particularly dedicate to my dear friends in the parish and neighbourhood of Olney, for whose use the hymns were originally composed ; as a testimony to the sincere love I bear them, and as a token of my gratitude to the Lord, and to them, for the comfort and satisfaction with which the discharge of my ministry among them has been attended.

The hour is approaching, and at my time of life cannot be very distant, when my heart, my pen, and my tongue, will no longer be able to move in their service. But I trust, while my heart continues to beat, it will feel a warm desire for the prosperity of their souls ; and while my hand can write and my tongue can speak, it will be the business and pleasure of life, to aim at promoting their growth and establishment in the grace of our God and Saviour. To this precious grace I commend them, and earnestly entreat them, and all who love his name, to strive mightily with their prayers to God for me, that I may be preserved faithful to the end, and enabled at last to finish my course with joy.

Olney, Bucks.,
Feb. 15, 1779.

John Newton."

So with all the groundwork done, and backed up by much prayer, John Newton published the 'Olney Hymns'.

The first copies were printed in July, 1779, and sold for 2s. 6d. each in hardback. They contained three hundred and forty eight hymns, sixty eight by Cowper, and the remaining two hundred and eighty by Newton.

Any initial doubts that anyone had about the wisdom of the project were soon dispelled when they saw the popularity of the new hymnbook. When the news of its release became known, Christian people, and Christian churches all wanted to buy copies. The original two thousand copies were soon sold out, and it was reprinted.

When copies of it reached the American continent it became even more in demand, and was reprinted many times.

Why was it such an instant success?

The answer to this question lies in the clarity and sincerity of the hymns.

They fulfilled the purpose for which they were published. To enhance public worship by plain people.

And each of the volume's three books, or sections, merits special attention.

Each contains treasures, some well-known, and some as yet undiscovered.

All awaiting exploration...

33

Do You Really, Really Love Me?

❖

SINCE A SUBSTANTIAL NUMBER OF THE HYMNS IN THE OLNEY HYMNBOOK WERE WRITTEN AS EXPOSITIONS OF BIBLE PASSAGES FOR THE GREAT HOUSE GATHERINGS, IT IS HARDLY SURPRISING THAT FORTY PER CENT OF THE TOTAL COLLECTION IS TO BE FOUND IN THE FIRST SECTION. 'HYMNS FORMED UPON SELECT PASSAGES OF SCRIPTURE.'

Some of these hymns have already been included in this book, but there are two other well-known and widely-sung hymns, one by each of the joint authors, that merit consideration.

John Newton penned many hymns of praise, of which one of the best known must be his description of Zion. The city of God.

This hymn, or perhaps poem, as it started out, was based on the words of Isaiah chapter 33, vs 20-21 :-

"Look upon Zion, the city of our solemnities: thine eyes shall see Jerusalem a quiet habitation, a tabernacle that shall not be taken down; not one of the stakes thereof shall ever be removed, neither shall any of the cords thereof be broken.

But there the glorious Lord will be unto us a place of broad rivers and streams; wherein shall go no galley with oars, neither shall any gallant ship pass thereby."

However, a probably better known Scripture in this hymn is the one which Newton used to give him his opening line, Psalm 87, v 3 :-

"Glorious things are spoken of thee, O city of God. Selah."

Throughout the hymn, Newton uses, and in the hymnbook, identifies, many Scriptural references.

It has endured as a wonderful expression of praise, confidence and assurance :-

> Glorious things of thee are spoken (c),
> Zion, city of our God !
> He, whose word cannot be broken,
> Formed thee for his own abode (d) :
> On the rock of ages founded (e),
> What can shake thy sure repose ?
> With salvation's walls surrounded (f)
> Thou mayest smile at all thy foes.
>
> See ! the streams of living waters
> Springing from eternal love (g) ;
> Well supply thy sons and daughters,
> And all fear of want remove :
> Who can faint while such a river

Ever flows their thirst t' assuage ?
Grace, which like the Lord, the giver,
Never fails from age to age.

Round each habitation hovering
See the cloud and fire appear (h) !
For a glory and a covering,
Shewing that the Lord is near :
Thus deriving from their banner
Light by night and shade by day ;
Safe they feed upon the Manna
Which he gives them when they pray.

Blest inhabitants of Zion,
Washed in the Redeemer's blood !
Jesus, whom their souls rely on,
Makes them kings and priests to God (i) :
'Tis his love his people raises
Over self to reign as kings
And as priests, his solemn praises
Each for a thank-offering brings.

Saviour, if of Zion's city
I through grace a member am ;
Let the world deride or pity,
I will glory in thy name :
Fading is the worldling's pleasure,
All his boasted pomp and show :
Solid joys and lasting treasure,
None but Zion's children know.

(Olney Hymns. Book 1. Hymn 60.)
(c) Psalm 87v.3 (d) Psalm 132 v.14 (e) Matthew 16 v.16
(f)Isaiah 26 v.1 (g)Psalm 46 v.4 (h) Isaiah 4 vs.5,6
(i) Revelation 1 v.6

'Formed upon select passages of Scripture', was how Newton had described this first 'book' in his introduction. He was certainly right in regard to, 'Glorious things of thee are spoken'.

The hymn is a complete and absorbing Bible study in itself!

Another hymn that has proved to be both an inspiration and a challenge to many as it has been sung down the years, is William Cowper's thought-provoking application of the Saviour's question to Peter in John 21 v.6. "Lovest thou me?"

It is interesting to note that Cowper begins the hymn by introducing the Lord, using the words that John exclaimed to his flustered friend Peter by the sea of Galilee almost two thousand years ago. "It is the Lord".

He then goes on to confront his readers , or singers, or himself, with the single pointed question of Christ, "Say, poor sinner, lovest thou me ?"

It is entirely fitting that this hymn should be included in the directly-based-on- Bible-verses section of the Olney hymnbook, for not only is it based on John chapter 21, but it also contains a number of allusions to Scripture passages. Although these are not specifically identified by Newton, who was left with the not inconsiderable task of compiling the collection, in the same way as he does with some of his own hymns, yet they must be instantly recognisable to anyone at all familiar with the Bible.

Take the third verse, for example. It is an almost complete paraphrase of Isaiah 49 v.15. Look :-

> *"Can a woman forget her sucking child, that she should not have compassion on the son of her womb ? yea, they may forget, yet will I not forget thee."*

On the purely human level, does one detect in this verse a cry from the anguished heart of the author? A lament for the lack of mother love of which he was deprived when so very young. Just a thought.

Yet another interesting, and somewhat unusual, approach adopted in this hymn is the use, twice, of direct speech. Cowper has Christ presenting His claims to us, in His own words. One section begins, and the other ends, with the point-blank challenge to our love.

Small wonder that the poet concludes the hymn by confessing the totally unresponsive nature of his own heart when measured against the love and grace of God.

It is in many modern hymnals. And has been often sung.

Read it again now, and sing it again in the future, with a deeper understanding.

A fuller appreciation :-

> Hark, my soul ! it is the Lord ;
> 'Tis thy Saviour, hear his word ;
> Jesus speaks, and speaks to thee ;
> "Say, poor sinner, lovest thou me?
>
> I delivered thee when bound,
> And when wounded, healed thy wound ;
> Sought thee wandering, set thee right,
> Turned thy darkness into light."
>
> Can a woman's tender care
> Cease, towards the child she bare ?
> Yes, she may forgetful be,
> Yet will I remember thee.
>
> "Mine is an unchanging love,
> Higher than the heights above ;
> Deeper than the depths beneath,
> Free and faithful, strong as death.

Thou shalt see my glory soon,
When the work of grace is done ;
Partner of my throne shalt be,
Say, poor sinner, lovest thou me?"

Lord it is my chief complaint,
That my love is weak and faint
Yet I love thee and adore,
Oh for grace to love thee more !

(Olney Hymns. Book 1. Hymn 118.)

It must have been wonderful to hear Rev. John Newton
explaining the spiritual application of these hymns to keenly-
interested Christians packed into the Great House for the
mid-week prayer meeting. In the good old early days.

The two authors did not only write hymns specifically to
expound passages of Scripture, though.There were other
occasions in the Christian calendar, and in the life of the church,
for which a new hymn would be appropriate. And they had
set such a high standard for themselves, and had become so
expert, that it was no problem.

34

For That Special Occasion

---------------- ❖ ----------------

JOHN NEWTON WAS ALWAYS READY TO GRASP ANY
OPPORTUNITY TO PREACH THE GOSPEL. TO PRESENT
THE CHRISTIAN MESSAGE TO HIS PARISHIONERS.

Special events in the annual calendar of the church usually
afforded larger-than-usual audinces and were therefore
chances not to be missed. And the creative curate didn't miss
them.

In the second section of the hymnbook he drew together
all the hymns that had been composed for, and used upon,
such special occasions.

Most of them are interesting and instructive, but two of
them that have not been already quoted, are significant. And
worthwhile reproducing in full.

As year upon year mellowed into autumn, Newton
observed the farmers in the fields by the Ouse as they toiled
away, gathering in their crops. It was, to him, a forceful
reminder of the recurring goodness of his God.

On contemplating the blessing and beauty of the harvest his mind was drawn to something else. The miracle of growth. Both physical and spiritual. Not only did a dying seed in an inhospitable field yield a fruitful crop of corn, but the Gospel seed, sown in a once-hardened heart, could produce an often-buffeted but ultimately-bountiful harvest.

So he wrote a hymn about it. And used it for harvest-thanks-giving.

When one considers this hymn alongside the others which are sung every year in produce-packed churches on October Sundays, it is surprising that it has not been more widely used. Perhaps it was not considered thankful enough. Too serious for a celebration, maybe.

Newton called it simply, 'Harvest'.

> See ! the corn again in ear !
> How the fields and valleys smile !
> Harvest now is drawing near
> To repay the farmer's toil :
> Gracious Lord, secure the crop,
> Satisfy the poor with food ;
> In thy mercy is our hope,
> We have sinned, but thou art good.
>
> While I view the plenteous grain
> As it ripens on the stalk ;
> May I not instruction gain,
> Helpful, to my daily walk ?
> All this plenty of the field
> Was produced from foreign seeds ;
> For the earth itself would yield
> Only crops of useless weeds.

Though, when newly sown, it lay
Hid awhile beneath the ground,
(Some might think it thrown away)
Now a large increase is found :
Though concealed, it was not lost,
Though it died, it lives again ;
Eastern storms, and nipping frosts,
Have opposed its growth in vain.

Let the praise be all the Lord's,
As the benefit is ours !
He, in seasons, still affords
Kindly heat, and gentle showers :
By his care the produce thrives
Waving o'er the furrowed lands ;
And when harvest-time arrives,
Ready for the reaper stands.

Thus in barren hearts he sows
Precious seeds of heavenly joy (t),
Sin, and hell, in vain oppose,
None can grace's crop destroy :
Threatened oft, yet still it blooms,
After many changes past,
Death, the reaper, when he comes,
Finds it fully ripe at last.

> (t) Hosea 14 v.7 Mark 4 vs.26-29.
> (Olney Hymns. Book 2. Hymn 36.)

Whether they were regular attenders for the other eleven months or not, the time of the year when most families in Olney made a big effort to get out to church was Christmas. Dark, dismal December evenings saw the church crowded with humble people, celebrating the coming into the world of the Son of God. In humble circumstances.

Again this was a challenge to Newton. He must compose something for the worshippers to learn. To sing. To 'tell'. To remember.

And he did.

One Christmas in the 1770's, John Newton introduced a new hymn to his congregation. To help them appreciate the marvel of the season. Emmanuel. "God with us."

That hymn still remains in a number of present-day hymnbooks. Not usually as a Christmas hymn, or carol, but as a hymn of praise and worship. Which it is :-

Praise For The Incarnation

Sweeter sounds than music knows
    Charm me, in EMMANUEL's name ;
All her hopes my spirit owes
    To his birth, and cross, and shame.

When he came the angels sang
    "Glory be to God on high !"
Lord, unloose my stammering tongue,
    Who should louder sing than I ?

Did the Lord a man become
    That he might the law fulfil,
Bleed and suffer in my room ;
    And canst thou, my tongue, be still ?

No! I must my praises bring,
    Though they worthless are, and weak ;
For should I refuse to sing
    Sure the very stones would speak.

O my Saviour, Shield, and Sun,
　　Shepherd, Brother, Husband, Friend,
Every precious name in one,
　　I will love thee without end.

(Olney Hymns. Book 2. Hymn 37.)

What infectious joy must have spread around the church in Olney as the congregation forgot for a moment the hardships that many of them called 'life', and sang, or at least repeated after their curate, those uplifting words,

'When he came the angels sang,
"Glory be to God on high!"'

And perhaps there were knowing smiles and nods-of-the-head when he read out the last verse. All those titles again ! They had heard them so often ! Were familiar with them by now!

But they loved them still.

Emmanuel. God with us.

The Word became flesh. To die on a cross.

To become their Saviour. Shepherd. Friend.

Wonderful, comforting concept.

35

Miscellaneous

❖

WHEN HE CAME TO CLASSIFY THE COLLECTION
OF HYMNS INTO SECTIONS, JOHN NEWTON DISCOV-
ERED THAT THERE WERE CERTAIN OF THE MANU-
SCRIPTS THAT HE HAD DECIDED TO INCLUDE IN THE
HYMNBOOK THAT JUST DIDN'T FIT IN PRECISELY
WITH HIS PREDEFINED CATEGORIES. THEY WEREN'T
BASED SPECIFICALLY ON PORTIONS OF SCRIPTURE.
NOR HAD THEY BEEN COMPOSED TO CELEBRATE
SOME SPECIAL EVENT OR SEASON. THERE WERE
OVER ONE HUNDRED COMPOSITIONS, INCLUDING
SOME SHORT ONE- AND TWO-VERSE HYMNS, WHICH
HE CONSIDERED WORTHY OF INCLUSION, BUT
WHICH WERE DIFFERENT FROM THE OTHERS IN
SOME PARTICULAR WAY.

So he created a section for them on their own. And called
them 'miscellaneous' hymns. They were a mixed-bag. Hymns

Allsorts. Comfort in conflict for Christians. Solemn addresses to sinners.

To demonstrate the diversity of type in the hymns which constitute the third 'book', and hence the problems of choice facing Newton as compiler of the Olney hymnbook, two of these miscellaneous hymns are here considered.

The first is by William Cowper.

Always a keen observer of Nature - the 'effect, whose cause is God' - the poet wrote a hymn in which he mentioned all of the four seasons in turn, identifying in each, and in the beauty of the dawn and the stillness of the evening, various simple but nonetheless beautiful, features that drew his alert mind and thankful soul, to worship his powerful God. And his loving, gentle Saviour.

He entitled it, appropriately, 'I Will Praise the Lord at All Times.' :-

> Winter has a joy for me ,
> While the Saviour's charm's I read,
> Lowly, meek, from blemish free,
> In the snow-drop's pensive head.
>
> Spring returns, and brings along
> Life-invigorating suns :
> Hark ! The turtle's plaintive song,
> Seems to speak his dying groans !
>
> Summer has a thousand charms,
> All expressive of his worth ;
> 'Tis his sun that lights and warms,
> His the air that cools the earth.
>
> What, has autumn left to say
> Nothing, of a Saviour's grace ?
> Yes, the beams of milder day
> Tell me of his smiling face.

Light appears with early dawn ;
While the sun makes haste to rise,
See his bleeding beauties drawn,
On the blushes of the skies.

Evening, with a silent pace,
Slowly moving in the west,
Shews an emblem of his grace,
Points to an eternal rest.

(Olney Hymns. Book 3. Hymn 83.)

One of John Newton's own hymns which he included in the final section of the hymnbook is a delightful blend of testimony to the goodness of God in his life, even during his wild and rebellious days, and his confidence in God for the future.

As a parish minister in Olney he encountered many problems. Difficult human problems. Poverty. Sickness. Lacemakers worried about their livelihood. Their future. The struggle to feed their families.

Some, no doubt, began to doubt their faith. Question their lot. Ask, "Why?"

This hymn was for them. As an encouragement to go on. To persevere, with their trust in God and His assurance of a brighter beyond. The prospect of heaven, and 'The conqueror's song'.

It is still in use in a few hymnbooks today, and has probably proved to be a spiritual stimulant to hundreds of struggling believers.

It is interesting to observe the nautical reference in this hymn. Newton never lost his love for the sea, and ships. They had become part of him. Could these lines have been the inspiration for the children's chorus, perhaps ?

"With Christ in the vessel,
We can smile at the storm,
As we go sailing home..."

Although intended as a general hymn of encouragement, and not based on any specific text of Scripture, the title the author gave this particular composition is drawn from Isaiah, chapter twelve :-

I Will Trust And Not Be Afraid.

Begone unbelief,
My Saviour is near,
And for my relief
Will surely appear :
By prayer let me wrestle,
And he will perform,
With Christ in the vessel,
I smile at the storm.

Though dark be my way,
Since he is my guide,
'Tis mine to obey,
'Tis his to provide ;
Though cisterns be broken,
And creatures all fail,
The word he has spoken
Shall surely prevail.

His love in time past
Forbids me to think
He'll leave me at last
In trouble to sink ;
Each sweet Ebenezer
I have in review,

Confirms his good pleasure
To help me quite through.

Determined to save,
He watched o'er my path,
When Satan's blind slave,
I sported with death ;
And can he have taught me
To trust in his name,
And thus far have brought me,
To put me to shame ?

Why should I complain
Of want or distress,
Temptation or pain ?
He told me no less :
The heirs of salvation,
I know from his word,
Through much tribulation
Must follow their Lord (u).

How bitter that cup,
No heart can conceive,
Which he drank quite up,
That sinners might live !
His way was much rougher,
And darker than mine ;
Did Jesus thus suffer,
And shall I repine ?

Since all that I meet
Shall work for my good,
The bitter is sweet,

And the med'cine is food ;
Though painful at present,
Will cease before long,
And then, oh how pleasant !
The conqueror's song (x) !

(u) Acts 14 v.22 (x) Romans 8 v.37
(Olney Hymns. Book 3. Hymn 37.)

The success of the Olney Hymnbook was a highlight of the summer of 1779 for John Newton. But he had become ever more aware that the days when his ministry, and indeed his presence, were appreciated in the Buckinghamshire town, had come to an end.

Opposition to him was increasing. Congregations in his church were decreasing.

The preacher was about to be called upon to prove that he believed in what he had been preaching.

The teacher was to be tested on what he had taught.

And the hymnwriter questioned on what he had written.

He had often preached that God was in control of the Christian's life. Difficult and trying times were all part of His master-plan...

He had sat with distressed parents or suffering parishioners and had read to them from Romans chapter 8 v.28 :-

"And we know that all things work together for good to them that love God, to them that are the called according to his purpose."

He had written that, 'The bitter is sweet,' and, 'The medicine is food'.

Now the storm clouds were gathering around himself.

Could he prove it all in practice?

He had patiently and successfully guided his friend William Cowper through a crisis in his life.

What was he going to do now, himself ?

36

'A Busy Idleness'

❖

JOHN NEWTON KNEW THAT HE MUST MOVE FROM
OLNEY. HE COULDN'T REMAIN THERE ANY LONGER.
IT WAS IMPOSSIBLE.

Though a forthright and earnest preacher, he was also a
very sensitive individual. He knew that he had been indis-
creet in the way he had handled things on more than one
occasion. Had made mistakes. Raised a few hackles. Been
responsible, at least in part, for bringing some of his troubles
upon himself.

Writing to William Bull in Newport Pagnell, he acknowl-
edged this, with his own peculiar brand of wit.

"The truth is," he avowed, "the next time I am young, and
begin to preach in a country place, I intend to do not just as I
did in Olney."

But what were his options? Where would he, indeed, where
could he go?

Again the generous and influential merchant, John Thornton had the answer. Having been aware for some time of the growing tide of opposition to Newton in Olney, and also knowing of the curate's own personal concerns about the situation, he came up with a solution.

There was a large Church of England in London, St. Mary Woolnoth in Lombard Street, which was perhaps the only one in the capital at that time with sympathies toward the steadily expanding Evangelical movement, and it was without a permanent minister.

John Thornton, who appreciated the tireless work and Bible-based teaching of Newton, arranged for him to be offered the position of minister at the church.

This offer pleased the by-now-unsettled curate. It was to him yet another evidence of the guiding hand of God in his life. He was pleased to accept.

Yet he and Mary would have one huge regret at moving from Olney. They would have to leave behind their close friends, William Cowper and Mary Unwin.

How were they ever going to tell them?

It was a rather subdued John and Mary who crossed the Guinea Field into Orchard Side that evening in late September, 1779. They had been rehearsing all day how best to break the news. Rephrasing it. Putting it this way and that.

In the event, Cowper and Mary Unwin, though rather upset at the probability of losing the almost daily contact they enjoyed with their dear friends, were very sensible about the whole affair. They knew something, but not all, of the mounting opposition to Newton in the town. And they had to admit that it would be a wise move for John. The prospect of the 'living' of a big London church could only be good for him. It would help him to become more widely known as a writer, and his talent for preaching the Gospel and expounding the

Scriptures would be used to bring challenge and comfort to much wider audiences.

Despite an acknowledgement of these obviously positive factors, they were all very sad. Each one of them was by now over fifty years of age, and none of them could contemplate the thought of a parting without some sense of gloom.

Although mental 'panic stations' had been Cowper's initial reaction, the poet consoled himself with the fact that London wasn't all that far away. The two men were both very diligent correspondents, so they could always write to one another. And indeed there was no reason why they shouldn't all visit each other on a regular basis.

They drank tea together in the parlour, and discussed the future for all of them, well into the night.

When they eventually retraced their steps across the Guinea Orchard the Newtons still had heavy hearts, but were in a strange sense somewhat relieved. The news was out. The ice broken.

On reaching his study, Newton summed up the whole evening's exchanges with the simple but succinct comment in his diary, "Dear Mrs. Unwin and Mr. Cowper feel concerned that we must be parted."

That parting took place in two stages.

John had to move to London to take the charge of his new church in January, 1780, and to find somewhere for he and Mary to live. Do some 'house-hunting'.

When he eventually found a suitable house in Charles Square, Hoxton, Mary joined him in February.

This move meant a big change for all of them

For John Newton and his wife it was a totally different environment from the relative tranquility of rural Olney. A place of 'much noise and smoke', was how Newton described the London of that day. It was, indeed, a turbulent place to which they had come.

There was political unrest about the war in the American colonies. There was social unrest amongst many of the unfortunate poor who were mercilessly manipulated by many of the unscrupulous rich. All kinds of crime were rife. And offenders were crowded into damp, unsanitary prisons. Disease was widespread.

To add to the troubles of the couple on taking up residence in the capital, it so happened that the congregation of St. Mary Woolnoth weren't altogether happy with their new minister at first. Their disquiet stemmed from the fact that they hadn't been given any say whatsoever in his appointment. Many of them had never heard of the man until they were informed that he was coming. So they didn't take him to their hearts at once. For many months he didn't receive any invitations to visit their homes. This annoyed him. It was so different from his Buckinghamshire parish where he had, at least in his early days there, been always welcome in the homes of the people.

This initial frosty reception by his own congregation, coupled with the combined opposition of the ministers of the other established churches in the city, who were unhappy with the appointment of an evangelical minister, must have led him to question the wisdom of the move to London many a time.

John and Mary missed Olney very much.

They longed again to watch the Ouse meander silently through the grassy meadows. And they would just love to hear the lowing of the cattle and the bleating of the sheep once more.

Writing to Betsy, who was at school in Northampton, John Newton recalled earlier, pleasant memories. "There are no pretty walks here amongst the trees and the fields", he lamented, "and no birds but such as are prisoners in iron cages, so I pity them for all their singing."

Olney missed them too.

It didn't take long for the townspeople to realize their loss, when it was too late. They didn't appreciate the abilities of the man they had, until they lost him ! Newton's replacement lasted a very short time in the church. He couldn't live up to the expectations of the congregation.

John Newton was just too hard an act to follow !

By far the keenest sense of loss, though, was felt by William Cowper and Mary Unwin. The Newtons' removal to London left a huge gap in the every-day, close-contact friendship of their lives. An awful aura of emptiness.

Since Mary Newton was the last to leave the Vicarage, Cowper wrote to her in early March, just after the final flit. The tone of his letter echoes that feeling of loneliness in the absence of his close friend, the curate :-

"... The Vicarage became a Melancholy Object, as soon as Mr. Newton had left it : When you left it, it became more melancholy : now it is actually occupied by another Family. Even I cannot look at it without being shocked. As I walked   in the Garden this Evening, I saw the Smoke issue from the Study Chimney, and said to myself, that used to be a sign that Mr. Newton was there, but it is so no longer ..."

As time progressed, however, they all came to terms with this new phase in their lives. A new pattern of relationships was established.

William Cowper corresponded regularly with both John and Mary.

His letters to John were of a general nature, ranging over a wide variety of topics. They kept him up to date with the gossip of Olney, whilst also passing comment on deeper matters both spiritual and political.

To Mary he wrote more specifically. Thanking her for the gifts of seafood that she sent him from the city, as she knew him to be a great lover of eating fish. And filling her in on all the trivialities of 'how his garden grew.' She had been delighted to discover that her new London home had a small garden to it, so she set about redesigning and restocking this little garden with great enthusism.

But she needed some new plants. And seeds.

And she knew who had them. Sir Cowper.

So she persuaded her husband to ask for them. Thus, in one of Newton's letters to their friends in Olney, he added across the top :-

> " *My dear will be much oblig'd to you for some suitable and seasonable furniture for her small garden. Roots and seeds and what you think proper. She says something about Curious seeds, as if there were some seeds that are not curious. But she wants to oblige a Gentleman with some "curious" seeds.*"

Both households had an unwritten argeement to spend the late hours on a Sunday evening writing letters to each other.

It worked, too. They all still felt they belonged as a unit, although separated by many miles. Though the parting had been painful, they were learning to live apart. Successfully.

Gradually, also, John Newton was accepted by the members of his congregation. And by many of the well-to-do in London society. His fame as the author of, 'An Authentic Narrative', soon spread, and people began to flock to St. Mary Woolnoth to hear him preach. Slowly but surely then, the invititations to visit in homes across the capital began to be received. Not only were these the homes of his parishioners. There were also invitations to call upon the homes of prominent businessmen and academics.

It wasn't all one way traffic, either. At first a trickle, and then a steady stream of people, came to his home in Hoxton for spiritual and moral counsel, as well.

Everybody seemed to like to listen to him.

He had so much to tell. About life at sea. About God's amazing grace. About life in a country parish. He had such a wealth of wisdom and experience.

And not only did he have so much to tell, but he had a quaint and witty way of telling it.

Just as he was beginning to become better known in the city, and was starting to be respected as a preacher of the Gospel and a teacher of the Scriptures, as well as an author and raconteur of some note, his friend in deepest Buckinghamshire enquired of him in a letter as to the progress of his life and work in London.

Newton's response says it all :-

> *"Indeed I live a strange life. It looks upon a review, only a busy idleness. My time is divided between running about to look on other people, and sitting at home like a tame Elephant or a Monkey for other people to come and look at me."!*

37

The Name And Fame Of A Poet

❖

WHILE LIFE WAS BECOMING MORE INTERESTING BY
THE DAY FOR NEWTON IN LONDON, NOTHING HAD
CHANGED ALL THAT MUCH BACK IN OLNEY.

William Cowper, temporarily disconcerted by John and
Mary's move to the capital, and still convinced that he had
permanently estranged himself from God, turned his fertile
mind to other pursuits.

Newton's letters always contained items designed to
encourage and reassure him spiritually, but Cowper found it
difficult to respond positively to such cheering counsel. In the
depths of winter, but not quite in the depths of despair, he
replied to one such letter, on 21st December, 1780, by stating :-

*"Your sentiments with respect to me, are exactly Mrs.
Unwin's. She, like you, is perfectly sure of my deliverance and often tells me so. I make but one Answer, and*

sometimes none at all. That Answer gives HER no
pleasure, and would give YOU as little. Therefore, at this
time, I suppress it..."

However, he did divulge to his faithful advisor and regular correspondent, later in that same letter, the source of one of his few pleasures in life :-

"... At this season of the year, & in this gloomy, uncomfortable climate, it is no easy matter for the owner of a mind like mine, to divert it from sad subjects, & fix it upon such as may minister to its amusement. Poetry, above all things, is useful to me in this respect. While I am held in pursuit of pretty images, or pretty ways of expressing them, I forget everything that is irksome, & , like a boy that plays truant, determine to avail myself of the present opportunity to be amused, & to put by the disagreeable recollection that I must after all, go home & be whipt again..."

Poetry. The writing of poetry. The pursuit and expression of pretty images.

This had become his lifeline. His escape hatch.

As his mental condition had stabilised during the late 1770's, William Cowper had returned to the writing of verse. Not hymns this time, but poems on a variety of subjects.

This interest in, and ability for, writing yet more poetry, combined with the publication of the Olney Hymns in 1779, which had brought Cowper's name and literary prowess to the attention of the general public, led to suggestions by Mrs. Unwin and some other friends, that he should consider publishing a book of poems.

Initially Cowper was rather reluctant. He just didn't think his work was good enough. To him, the writing of poetry was a hobby. A pleasant release from moods of melancholy. And as for his poems, he considered them merely 'trifles'.

When William Unwin commented favourably on his work once, Cowper responded, "I have no more right to the name of a Poet, than a maker of mousetraps has to that of an Engineeer. Such a talent in verse as mine, is like a child's rattle, very entertaining to the trifler that uses it, and very disagreeable to all beside."

He was to be proved wrong on that one.

In the early years of the 1780's the void left by the removal of the Newtons from Olney was in part filled by the composition of more, and yet more poetry.

Encouraged by Mary Unwin, he wrote a series of long poems. These were on religious or moral subjects and were thoroughly interspersed with references to Christian themes and Scripture passages.

His description of God's salvation and the proud sinner's rejection of it , in 'Truth ', has often been quoted by speakers who were possibly unaware of its source :-

"...Oh, how unlike the complex works of man,
Heaven's easy, artless, unencumbered plan !...
It stands like the cerulean arch we see,
Majestic in its own simplicity.
Inscribed above the portal, from afar
Conspicious as the brightness of a star,
Legible only by the light they give,
Stand the soul-quickening words — BELIEVE, AND LIVE.
Too many, shocked at what should charm them most,
Despise the plain direction and are lost.
Heaven on such terms ! they cry with proud disdain,
Incredible, impossible, and vain ! —
Rebel because 'tis easy to obey,
And scorn for its own sake the gracious way..."

Probably not so well-known, but certainly equally as powerful, is the description of 'the way of the cross', with which he concludes, 'The Progress of Error' :-

"...But if the wanderer his mistake discern,
Judge his own ways, and sigh for a return,
Bewildered once, must he bewail his loss
For ever and for ever ? No ! The Cross !..
There no delusive hope invites despair,
No mockery meets you, no deception there ;
The spells and charms that blinded you before,
All vanish there, and fascinate no more.
I am no preacher, let this hint suffice —
The cross, once seen, is death to every vice ;
Else He that hung there suffered all his pain,
Bled, groaned and agonised, and died in vain."

Soon the piles of hand-written long poems began to grow around Orchard Side. 'Hope', 'Charity', 'Conversation', and 'Retirement' had been added to those already mentioned above. Submitting to the pressure from his friends who recognised the value and quality of the compositions, Cowper finally agreed, with a shy pleasure, to allow his long poems to go forward for publication.

This first collection of poems, entitled, "Poems, by William Cowper, Esq., of the Inner Temple", was published in 1782.

John Newton was delighted to be asked to write the preface to this book, and in it he recounted something of Cowper's life until that time. He had this to say of their companionship:-

"...*The good hand of God was providing for me one of the principal blessings of my life ; a friend and a counsellor,*

*in whose company for almost seven years, though we were
seldom seven successive waking hours separated, I always
found new pleasure. A friend who was not only a comfort
to myself, but a blessing to the affectionate poor people
among whom I then lived."*

Newton explained that he understood Cowper's purpose
in the writing of these "large poems", as he described them,
to be, aiming "to communicate his own perception of the truth,
beauty, and influence of the religion of the Bible."

Ever willing to avail himself of every opportunity to
proclaim the message of the Gospel, by whatever means, he
ended his preface with a testimony in the first person plural,
embracing, presumably, the poet and himself :-

*"We are now certain, that the Gospel of Christ is the power
of God unto salvation, to every one that believeth. It has
reconciled us to God, and to ourselves, to our duty, and
our situation. It is the balm and cordial of the present life,
and a sovereign antidote against the fear of death...*

JOHN NEWTON

*Charles Square, Hoxton,
February 18, 1782 "*

Cowper was now in print. His first volume of poetry.

When this book became available, late in 1782, it received
modest praise from most of the secular reviewers, some
commenting favourably on the homely originality of Cowper's
poetic style. Others, however, were critical, not of the style,
but of the content of the work. It was simply "too religious"
for them.

One of the classic, and much-appreciated-by-Christians, examples of the Scriptural nature of these poems, is the description, in 'Conversation', of 'the two on the way to Emmaus'. (Luke 24). In it, Cowper puts forward the discourse of the distraught disciples as a model of meaningful conversation :-

"... It happened on a solemn eventide,
Soon after He that was our surety died,
Two bosom friends, each pensively inclined,
The scene of all those sorrows left behind,
Sought their own village, busied as they went,
In musings worthy of the great event :
They spake of Him they loved, of Him whose life,
Though blameless had incurred perpetual strife,
Whose deeds had left, in spite of hostile arts,
A deep memorial graven on their hearts.
The recollection, like a vein of ore,
The farther traced, enriched them still the more ;
They thought Him, and they justly thought Him, one
Sent to do more tnan He appeared t' have done ;
To exalt a people, and to place them high
Above all else, and wondered He should die.
Ere yet they brought their journey to an end,
A stranger joined them, courteous as a friend,
And asked them with an engaging air,
What their affliction was, and begged a share.
Informed, He gathered up the broken thread,
And, truth and wisdom gracing all He said,
Explained, illustrated, and searched so well,
The tender theme on which they choose to dwell,
That reaching home, The night, they said, is near,
We must not now be parted, sojourn here —

The new acquaintance soon became a guest,
And made so welcome at their simple feast,
He blessed the bread, but vanished at the word,
And left them both exclaiming, 'Twas the Lord !
Did not our hearts feel all He deigned to say,
Did they not burn within us by the way ?
Now their's was converse such as it behoves
Man to maintain, and such as God approves :
Their views indeed were indistinct and dim,
But yet successful, being aimed at Him..."

While Cowper was beginning to enjoy the fame of being a published poet, in his own right, he was also beginning to enjoy the company of another much younger woman, to whom he had been introduced. She was the sister-in-law of the minister of the nearby vilage of Clifton Reynes, and a widow.

She was Lady Austen. An attractive, intelligent woman. And an Evangelical.

The two had many similar interests and struck up a close friendship. "Sister Anne", as Cowper used to call her, was soon to become an inspiration to him in his writng. He composed the poem, ' The Loss of The Royal George', commemerating the tragic sinking, in an unusual accident, of the flagship of the British fleet at Spithead on 29th August, 1782, for her. About eight hundred people were drowned in this tragedy, but since Lady Austen 'wanted words to the March in Scipio', so that she could sing whilst playing her harp, Cowper wrote for her:-

"Toll for the brave - the Brave that are no more -
All sunk beneath the wave, fast by their native shore -..."

To pass a gloomy winter evening, Lady Austen told William and Mary a funny story that she had heard in London. It was about a man called John Gilpin who set out to celebrate his twentieth wedding anniversary with his wife, but ended up getting a lot more than he had bargained for !

Cowper thought the story so hilarious that he spent the next four days retelling it in verse. He gave his poem the curious but cumbersome title of, 'The Diverting History of John Gilpin ; Showing How He Went Farther Than He Intended, And Came Safe Home Again.'

This poem became instantly popular. It was soon being recited for amusement at all sorts of public gatherings across the country. Some critics accord this poem the title of 'Cowper's most famous' composition. Christian people would have a different idea though. Surely more people have either read, quoted or sung,

> "There is a fountain filled with blood
> Drawn from Emmanuel's veins..."

than have ever even heard of John Gilpin !

It was Lady Austen, too, who suggested to him that he should attempt to write a longer poem in free verse, rather than in rhyming couplets like his earlier moral poems. She even proposed a number of subjects to start him off.

Cowper selected 'The Sofa', and began. To 'sing the sofa.'

Surprisingly, 'Sister Anne' soon became the victim of her own desire to assist the by-now-acclaimed but still-oft-depressed poet. He was so busy writing away night and day, following up all her exciting ideas, that he didn't have the same time for her ! Long walks in the country and long chats in the parlour at Orchard Side became more infrequent. And also, Cowper began to suspect that the mother figure who had cared for him so selflessly for many years, Mary Unwin, was becoming somewhat jealous of their relationship.

So he made, what for him was a very painful decision, and in the spring of 1784 wrote Lady Austen "a very tender yet resolute letter", terminating the relationship.

But she had started him out on what was to become the most prolonged single endeavour of his poetry-writing career. It was a long poem in six books, originally all called 'The Sofa ' but Cowper later renamed it ,'The Task'.

Some critics have implied that after Newton left Olney Cowper showed no further interest in writing 'religious verse'. That is not the case.

The sentiments he expressed in the last lines of,'The Winter Morning Walk', Book 5 of 'The Task', would contradict any such suggestion. Referring to God he wrote :-

"Thou art the source and centre of all minds
Their only point of rest, eternal Word !
From Thee departing, they are lost and rove
At random without honour, hope, or peace.
From Thee is all that soothes the life of man,
His high endeavour, and his glad success,
His strength to suffer and his will to serve
But oh, Thou bounteous Giver of all good,
Thou art of all Thy gifts Thyself the crown !
Give what Thou canst, without Thee we are poor ;
And with Thee rich, take what Thou wilt away."

When the second volume of his poems, including 'The Task' and 'John Gilpin' was published in 1785, it received immediate and general approval. William Cowper, Esq., of the Inner Temple, had been accorded the fame of a poet.

So he could justly claim 'the name of a Poet'.

But despite his feelings of despair about his relationship with God, his Heavenly Father hadn't deserted him. He was still a Christian too.

It shone out of his work..

In a letter to John Newton after the publication of 'The Task', he summed up his own personal evaluation of the poem by saying that God had enabled him to 'bring much truth out of much trifle'.

He was right about that.

38

'Sweet Meat Has Sour Sauce'

—————————————— ❖ ——————————————

IN DECEMBER, 1785, AN ANXIOUS YOUNG MAN CREPT
FURTIVELY UP TO THE DOOR OF THE VESTRY OF
ST. MARY WOOLNOTH CHURCH AND HANDED IN A
LETTER, ADDRESSED TO REV. JOHN NEWTON. THE
LETTER CONTAINED A REQUEST FOR AN APPOINT-
MENT, 'TO HAVE SOME SERIOUS CONVERSATION'.
THE WRITER ALSO STRESSED THAT ANY MEETING
SHOULD BE IN PRIVATE BECAUSE OF HIS PUBLIC
IMAGE.

It was like Nicodemus by day.

John Newton was pleased to grant the young man his
request, and set a date for a private meeting in his home in
Charles Square.

When the appointed time came around and the person who
had asked for the interview turned up, John Newton was
confronted with someone very concerned and confused. His

name was William Wilberforce, Member of Parliament for Hull, and a personal friend of the Prime Minister, William Pitt.

In the secure seclusion of Newton's study the mixed-up twenty-six year old M.P. poured out his story.

He was a Christian, having trusted in Christ as Saviour earlier in life. But he was a very frustrated and feeble Christian. He had lost the joy he once had in the Lord, long ago. Since coming to live and work in London he had become involved in the busy life of a conscientious Member of Parliament, and as an intellectual and conversationalist had become a desirable companion in fashionable London society.

But he just wasn't happy.

He felt that he was getting nowhere in life. Going nowhere fast. It was all frothy bubbles. When he should have felt satisfied and fulfilled he felt empty and disheartened.

John Newton sat silently. Pensive. Taking it all in.

When William Wilberforce had finished pouring out his heart to his sympathetic listener he came to the crux of the matter. His reason for seeeking the reverend gentleman out in the first place.

What would Mr. Newton, who was by now a respected confidant and counsellor of many of the capital's rich and famous, suggest that he should do?

Leave politics and return to Yorkshire? Go to a College somewhere and train for the Christian ministry? Or what?

Newton thought it all over for a few minutes, then gave his opinion.

Recognising in the earnest young man before him someone who had not only wealth and position but also wisdom and potential, he didn't advise any wildly dramatic course of action.

His first recommendation to Wilberforce was that he get back to God. Reopen the long-left-idle lines of communication with his Heavenly Father. And stand firmly for and witness boldly to his faith, wherever he found himself. This, in itself, would be a diffcult test for the young M.P. Easy enough for Newton to talk. Everybody knew him, and what he stood for. He hadn't ever left anybody in any doubt about that.

It would be a big, bold step for Wilberforce, though.

But he was prepared to take it.

Secondly, Newton suggested that instead of running round in an endless circle of social engagements, it would be much more rewarding, both mentally and spiritually, if he could fix his eye on some worthwhile goal for his life, and run in a straight line towards it.

None of this required Wilberforce to move out of his present social set. It merely required that he establish himself on a different level within it.

After a number of secret meetings, he saw the wisdom of the older man's advice. And acted upon it. He returned, in humility, to God. Seeking forgiveness, he pledged himself to the service of his heavenly Master.

Soon he didn't care who saw him come and go from the great man's house in Charles Square. He had an aim in life, now. He called it, initially, 'the reformation of manners'. His idea was to lay the claims of the Christian gospel, both spiritual and social before the aristocracy of the land, who had remained largely unaffected by the Evangelical revival under Whitefield and the Wesleys.

How should he go about it though? Where should he start?

He needn't have worried on that score. God was well ahead of him. He had been preparing the ground for His servant, for the previous twenty years, or so.

Since the early 1760's there had developed in England a rising feeling of disquiet about what had become known as the African Slave Trade. An increasing number of sincere people, many of them Dissenters, began to regard this business as immoral. Barbaric, almost. But they had no influence. No political 'clout'. Nobody took any notice of them, and their well-meaning ideas...

Then, enter William Wilberforce, M.P. Accepted. Respected. And fluent.

A restored Christian with a real concern.

He heard of the anxieties of a number of these people, and arranged to meet them. The up-until-that-moment ineffective anti-slavery activists were delighted to enlist the support of the yearning-to-be-effective Member of Parliament. And they voiced their desire for some sort of action, to him, again and again.

Wilberforce already knew something of the slave trade from the old ex-slave trader himself, John Newton. He admitted later that he had never been in Newton's company for more than half-an-hour without him expressing regret, at some stage, for the folly of his ways. Even as a young, but immature Christian.

These concerned people realised that if the slave trade was ever to be stopped, immediate action would have to be taken. And a united front presented.

So, on 22nd May, 1787, twelve men formed the Society for the Abolition of Slavery. The leader of, and public spokesman for, this Society, was none other than William Wilberforce.

Now the newly-formed Society needed factual evidence for the advancement of its campaign. And some method of bringing their deep concerns to the public notice.

They needed well-known names. Public figures. People of influence and ability.

It didn't take them long, either, to discover that they had two more, in addition to William Wilberforce.

Their names were John Newton and William Cowper.

Newton was ideally suited to champion their cause.

He was the only person that they could think of who had 'hands on' experience of the African Slave Trade. He knew about buying and selling slaves. About the conditions on board the ships on the Middle Passage. And to add to his suitability he had also worked as a Tide Surveyor in the port of Liverpool.

He knew the whole business inside-out.

By now his conscience was becoming more and more stirred about his own personal involvement in the trade. The voices of the abolitionists had begun to echo around in the depths of his sensitive soul.

So he volunteered to write an article outlining the evils of the SlaveTrade, as he saw them.

This very well-written and well-reasoned article was published as a pamphlet with the simple title, 'Thoughts on the African Slave Trade', and had a moving effect on all who read it.

In it, Newton introduced his former occupation as, 'business at which my heart now shudders'. His argument then progressed, cleverly, from the detrimental effect which the Slave Trade was having on the English sailors, many of whom never returned from futile attempts to cross the vast Atlantic Ocean in tiny ships, to the conditions aboard those ships and the treatment which was meted out to the human cargoes in transit.

Its publication presented a strong case to the country. Three thousand copies of it were printed, and 'dispersed about the Kingdom'. Indeed, 'Thoughts on the African Slave Trade', caused such consternation amongst Members of Parliament, and aroused such opposition from wealthy merchants and shipowners, who all had a vested interest in the continuance of the trade, that Newton was summoned, in 1788, to give evidence on the matter to the Privy Council. He was personally introduced to this meeting by William Pitt, who knew him to be a friend of William Wilberforce.

So the case for the abolition of the Slave Trade was at last being heard at the very highest level in the land. Deep in the corridors of power.

That, however, was not where the bulk of the people in the country were. They were the plain, ordinary people. In the streets of the towns and cities. Up the lanes and round the villages of the country areas.

They needed a different kind of message. By a different method.

And for that the Society for the Abolition of Slavery approached William Cowper, Esq., of The Inner Temple. Poet.

Aware of the tremendous success of the poem, 'John Gilpin', which had provided amusement for many at the time, they asked him if he would consider writing a few 'street ballads' in the same style, to be sung or recited in the streets and clubs. To bring their message, in easily remembered poetic form, to the mass of the population.

Cowper, though appalled at the stories about the traffic in slaves which he had heard often from his friend, John Newton, wasn't too keen at first. Being such a kind and gentle person himself, he just couldn't bear to contemplate the suffering of others.

Someone else, however, crossed his path at that time and had a positive influence upon him in this regard. Her name was Lady Hesketh.

By 1788, when the requests for the street ballads came to Cowper, two things had happened in his life.

The first was that he also had changed house. Mary Unwin and he had moved from Olney to the village of Weston Underwood, just two miles out of the town. There they took up residence in Weston Lodge, on the Weston Hall estate, which was owned by the Throckmortons, a well-to-do and highly respected Roman Catholic family. Cowper's developing friendship with the Throckmortons irritated Newton, perhaps through jealousy, and he wrote a number of uncharacteristically bitter letters on the subject. Though Newton's harsh and uncompromising attitude caused Cowper much anxiety for quite a while, the matter was, thankfully, eventually peacefully resolved.

The cruel communications from London caused the 'storms that' Cowper 'so much dreaded' to gather again on the horizon of his life, and in his fickle mind. All when he should have had so much to cheer him.

His two published collections of poetry had sold extremely well, and a new book, combining both of them into one larger volume was being planned. And the story of the hapless London merchant, John Gilpin, had made William Cowper a household name.

This growing renown caused many of his former friends to contact him again. One such was his cousin, Lady Harriet Hesketh. When she heard of William's fame, she renewed the contact, which had been allowed to lapse for many years, by turning up at Orchard Side.

She backed the move to Weston Underwood, when she witnessed the state of disrepair into which the house on the Market Square had fallen. But she also encouraged her talented cousin in another way, too. In his writing.

Being sympathetic to the cause of the Society for the Abolition of Slavery, and recognizing that the poet needed some mental stimulation to brighten his gloomy spirit, she urged him to respond to the request he had received. And write some 'street ballads'.

Cowper, pleased at her interest in his work, agreed to give it a try.

And he wrote four. All in the same year. 1788.

One of them Cowper called, 'Sweet Meat Has Sour Sauce', a title designed to highlight the contrast of the sweetmeats , such as sugar and rum, on the wealthy Englishman's table, and the bitter cost at which they were obtained.The abolitionists didn't like this poem as it was written in a rather witty style, and was therefore considered "too light" to serve the purpose for which it was supposed to be written.

Two of the others, 'The Morning Dream', and 'Pity for Poor Africans', were printed and probably sung, but they didn't become widely known.

The most famous of the four ballads, and the piece of Cowper's writing that became second in popularity, only to 'John Gilpin', in the poet's lifetime, was 'The Negro's Complaint'.

In it he pleaded the slave's entitlement to equality of treatment, regardless of the colour of his skin, and attempted to counter the argument being put forward by some, that God would not condemn the Slave Trade because through it, 'poor Africans' would somehow, or at sometime or another, come to learn about Him.

To appreciate the argument of the poem it must be quoted in full :-

The Negro's Complaint.

Forced from home and all its pleasures,
    Afric's coast I left forlorn ;
To increase a stranger's treasures,
    O'er the raging billows borne.
Men from England bought and sold me,
    Paid my price in paltry gold ;
But though slave they have enrolled me,
    Minds are never to be sold.

Still in thought as free as ever,
    What are England's rights, I ask,
Me from my delights to sever,
    Me to torture, me to task?
Fleecy locks and black complexion
    Cannot forfeit nature's claim ;
Skins may differ, but affection
    Dwells in black and white the same.

Why did all-creating Nature
    Make the plant for which we toil ?
Sighs must fan it, tears must water,
    Sweat of ours must dress the soil.
Think, ye masters, iron-hearted,
    Lolling at your jovial boards,
Think how many backs have smarted
    For the sweets your cane affords.

Is there, as ye somtimes tell us,
    Is there One who reigns on high ?
Has he bid you buy and sell us,
    Speaking from His throne, the sky ?
Ask him, if your knotted scourges,
    Matches, blood-extorting screws,
Are the means that duty urges
    Agents of His will to use.

Hark ! He answers ! - wild tornadoes
    Strewing yonder sea with wrecks,
Wasting towns, plantations, meadows,
    Are the voice with which He speaks.
He, forseeing what vexations
    Afric's sons should undergo,
Fixed their tyrants habitations
    Where His whirlwinds answer, "No !"

By our blood in Afric wasted,
  Ere our necks received the chain ;
By the miseries that we tasted,
  Crossing in your barks the main ;
By our sufferings, since ye brought us
  To the man-degrading mart,
All sustained by patience, taught us
  Only by a broken heart !

Deem our nation brutes no longer,
  Till some reason ye shall find
Worthier of regard and stronger
  Than the colour of our kind.
Slaves of gold, whose sordid dealings
  Tarnish all your boasted powers,
Prove that you have human feelings
  Ere you proudly question ours !

Strong stuff ! But it served its purpose.

It was printed, distributed and sung.

Then it was reprinted, distributed and sung.

People began to get the message.

And the combination of the tireless efforts of William Wilberforce and the abolitionist lobby, Newton's 'Thoughts on the African Slave Trade', and Cowper's powerful ballads, had the desired outcome.

In 1807 an Act was passed in Parliament forbidding the landing of slaves in all British colonies after March 1st, 1808.

But only two out of the three of them lived to see it...

39

In Peace At Last

❖

AS THE FAME OF WILLIAM COWPER SPREAD ACROSS
ENGLAND, AN INCREASING NUMBER OF VISITORS
BEGAN ARRIVING IN OLNEY AND WESTON
UNDERWOOD, HOPING FOR AN OPPORTUNITY
TO GET A GLIMPSE OF, OR PERHAPS EVEN A CONVER-
SATION WITH, THE CELEBRATED BUT AGEING POET.
SO IT CAME AS NO SURPRISE, WHEN, ONE DAY IN
JANUARY, 1790, MARY INFORMED COWPER THAT A
YOUNG CAMBRIDGE UNDERGRADUATE WOULD
LIKE TO MEET HIM.

Occasionally, when he was totally engrossed in some
literary project or other, the busy writer resented such inter-
ruptions, but since he loved to converse with people of learning, he was usually pleased to welcome his visitors.

As it so happened, he was certainly delighted to see this
particular one.

For they struck up a friendship that winter afternoon which endured until the day of Cowper's death.

The shy young man who had made his way to the door of Weston Lodge introduced himself as, "John Johnson from Norfolk. The grandson of Roger Donne."

William Cowper was absolutely thrilled. This was his first contact with the Donne side of the family for nearly thirty years ! "Johnny from Norfolk", as the poet was soon to nickname his second-cousin, was welcomed with open arms. And they talked and talked for hours. About Cambridge. About poetry. But most of all about 'the Norfolk connection'. Cowper had to get caught up on all the family news of more than twenty five years !

As the evening wore on and they were nowhere nearly finished, young John was persuaded to stay overnight. That gave them the chance to talk all through the next day as well!

John Johnson soon became a regular visitor to Weston Underwood.

His highly intelligent and deeply caring second-cousin discussed a wide variety of topics with him. Just as John Newton had become spiritual counsellor to William Wilberforce, so William Cowper became spiritual counsellor to John Johnson. It was as a direct result of Cowper's witness and testimony that the young Johnson became a committed Christian, and later a minister of the Gospel.

Meanwhile, repaired relationships between Cowper and his London friend led to a promise in a letter from Newton, during a particularly harsh winter, that he and Mary would visit Olney and Weston to call upon all their old friends in the spring.

Cowper was so excited at the prospect of meeting the Newtons in person again that he wrote a poem to express his delight, and enclosed it with his reply.

In two of the verses the warmth of Cowper's feeling bursts forth from the words.

From, 'To the Reverend Mr. Newton. An Invitation into the Country.' :-

> Old Winter, halting o'er the mead,
>   Bids me and Mary mourn ;
> But lovely Spring peeps o'er his head,
>   And whispers your return.
>
> And if a tear that speaks regret
>   Of happier times appear,
> A glimpse of joy that we have met
>   Shall shine, and dry the tear.

By this time, however, both Cowper and Mary Unwin were beginning to show their age. Mary suffered two strokes within six months in late-1791-early 1792. This was a serious blow to the poet's ever unstable state of mind. As he watched the deterioration in the health of the mother-figure in his life, it drew from his pen the pathetic, 'To Mary'.

In it he described his faithful housekeeper, her face permanently paralysed and her skill as a needlewoman finished. He held himself at least partly responsible for her condition. Six of the original fourteen verses will suffice to echo the despairing mood of the poet :-

> Thy spirits have a fainter flow,
> I see thee daily weaker grow; -
> 'Twas my distress that brought thee low,
>   My Mary !
>
> Thy needles, once a shining store,
> For my sake rustless heretofore,
> Now rust disused, and shine no more,
>   My Mary !

Thy indistinct expressions seem
Like language uttered in a dream :
Yet me they charm, whate'er the theme,
              My Mary !

Thy silver locks, once auburn bright,
Are still more lovely in my sight
Than golden beams of orient light,
              My Mary !

But ah ! by constant heed I know,
How oft the sadness that I show
Transforms thy smiles to looks of woe,
              My Mary !

And should my future lot be cast
With much resemblance of the past,
Thy worn-out heart will break at last,
              My Mary !

In 1793, Lady Hesketh came to visit the poet at Weston Underwood ,and when she witnessed the terrible state of his health, and realized that Mary Unwin was long past being able to care for herself, not to mention her famous cousin, she stayed.

And she remained, caring for the both of them, for the next two years.

This was not an easy task. William Cowper became very depressed again, early in 1794, and refused to cooperate with anybody, and Mary was totally incapable of doing anything.

In 1795, Lady Hesketh also took ill under the strain and the ever attentive John Johnson recognised that changes would have to be made. Something would have to be done. So he arranged for Cowper and Mary Unwin to be moved to his home county, Norfolk, where he would take responsibility for their care.

Perplexed at having to leave Olney and Weston, where he had spent so many happy days, Cowper wrote the following words on a window shutter at Weston Lodge:-

"Farewell, dear scenes, forever closed to me ;
Oh, for what sorrows must I now exchange ye !".

Then he left, with his Mary, and John Johnson, for the arduous three day coach journey into Norfolk, where John had arranged accommodation for them in East Dereham.

On December 17, 1796, the event which Cowper had dreaded for many years, happened. He lost Mary Unwin, who had been his faithful companion, for half of his life. She passed away, to be with Christ.

The poet cried out in anguish, when he was brought in to see her body, cold and silent in death, but after leaving the bedroom that night, such was the disturbed state of his mind, that he never mentioned her again.

Cowper's physical and mental condition continued to worsen.

In 1799, he wrote his last original poem, called 'The Castaway'. In it he told the story of a seaman lost overboard from one of Anson's ships, over fifty years before. His feelings of deep melancholy and a sense of despair led him to declare himself, "whelmed in deeper gulfs than he".

A year later, on 25th April, 1800, William Cowper, Esq., of The Inner Temple, talented Christian poet and hymnwriter, died peacefully. His struggles of mind and body were over. John Johnson, who had been with him right to the end, described the expression which came over his countenance at his passing as, "one of calmness and composure, mingled, as it were, with holy surprise."

Any wonder?!

Despite his firmly held notion that God had rejected him, he had just been proved wrong ! The God who had given him peace in his soul, in Dr. Cotton's Asylum, way back in 1764, had never left him. And now, to prove it, He had just transported that soul to His eternal home of peace and rest. Heaven.

Willam Cowper had seen his Lord !

After his death, a manuscript was discovered in which he had begun, but did not appear to have finished, a hymn. This hymn was finished by someone else, and is now included in many hymnals, attributed to Cowper.

The four verses which the poet did write, express beautifully the longing of a Christian heart, tired of the toils and trials of this world. A desire which was realized for him, that April evening :-

> To Jesus, the Crown of my Hope,
>   My soul is in haste to be gone ;
> O bear me, ye cherubim, up,
>   And waft me away to His throne !
>
> My Saviour, whom absent I love,
>   Whom, not having seen I adore ;
> Whose name is exalted above
>   All glory, dominion, and power ;
>
> Dissolve thou the bond that detains
>   My soul from her portion in Thee,
> And strike off the adamant chains,
>   And make me eternally free.
>
> When that happy era begins,
>   When arrayed in thy beauty I shine,
> Nor pierce any more, by my sins
>   The bosom on which I recline ;

The bond had been dissolved.
His soul was free.
And with Christ. Forever.
In peace. At last.

40

All Packed Up And Ready To Go

❖

IN THE LATE 1780'S JOHN AND MARY NEWTON
MOVED INTO THE CENTRE OF LONDON, TAKING UP
RESIDENCE IN 6, COLMAN STREET BUILDINGS, CLOSE
TO LOMBARD STREET AND ST. MARY WOOLNOTH
CHURCH.

Mary had taken ill and it was decided that it would be more
convenient for everyone, to be close to John's church, and to
have easy access to medical attention.

It was in this house in Colman Street that John Newton
attended his beloved Mary until she died. Towards the end
Mary became extremely weak, and was confined to bed for
months. Her devoted husband only left her bedside to preach
in the church, returning to be with her again as soon as possible.

On 15th December, 1790, John was leaning over her,
candle in hand, when her breathing stopped. It was so much

better for her, he knew, but it was a heart-breaking blow for him. They had enjoyed forty happy years of married life together. The tough old ex-seaman wept silently as a looked over at the bedside table. There lay Mary's well-marked Bible, and beside it her equally well-annotated copy of The Olney Hymns.

The funeral service was conducted by Newton himself, using as his text the passage that Cowper had paraphrased in, 'Sometimes a light surprises the Christian while he sings', Habakkuk 3 vs. 17-18. During his lifetime he had never spoken on that particular portion of Scripture, saving it, he often said, "For my dear's funeral, should she precede me".

Shortly after the funeral, though he missed his wife dreadfully, Newton became very active again. Both preaching and travelling. When caring friends offered to undertake his preaching duties for him, at least for a while, he invariably replied, "Dr. Pulpit is my best physician".

After Mary's death, Betsy came to live in 6, Colman Street to care for the man she delighted to call, "my father." This was good for the ageing preacher. Betsy helped entertain the many callers to the home, and encouraged Newton to travel extensively all over the country, preaching and visiting.

One such visit in 1792 was to Olney. His first and main call was to Weston Underwood, to see his old friend the poet, and Mary Unwin, who was by that time terribly paralysed. Although he enjoyed a day with Cowper, reviewing the past, he never returned to the Buckinghamshire town. The sight of the vicarage, and the garden from which Mary had derived such delight, the Church where he had so often preached, the Great House where he had expounded his own and Cowper's hymns to captive audiences, and Orchard Side, was all too much for him.

He never went back.

Although becoming increasingly both deaf and blind, John Newton spent the last years of the eighteenth century in a busy round of teaching, preaching, interviewing, writing, and counselling. All this activity served to help keep his mind off the big gap in his life after the death of Mary. Speaking to William Wilberforce about it in the late 90's he said, "God has healed the wound. But the scar remains".

In 1799, Newton received a sad letter from the one who had been such an inspiration to him nearly thirty years earlier. After recalling the happy days they had shared together in Olney, Cowper closed his letter, "Adieu, dear Sir, whom in those days I called dear friend, with feelings that justified the appellation."

It was sad, but certainly fitting, that this, the last letter the poet ever wrote, was to his close friend and spiritual confidant, the once-upon-a-time curate of Olney.

On hearing of Cowper's death in 1800, Newton wrote a touching tribute to him. In it, he told of how his friend had been, "a great blessing to the Lord's poor and afflicted people of Olney".

He then went on to give a wonderful description of Cowper the Christian :-

> *"... The wisdom which is from above, which is pure and peaceable, gentle and easy to be entreated, full of mercy and good works, without partiality and without hypocrisy, possessed and filled his heart. The wonders and riches of redeeming love, as manifested by the glorious gospel of the blessed God, were the food of his soul, the source of his joys, the habitual subject of his study, and suggested the leading topics of his conversation. Like the apostle, he was determined to know nothing comparatively but Jesus Christ and Him crucified, and to do nothing but in dependence upon His strength..."*

In 1801, Newton, by then seventy-six years old, suffered a further blow. Betsy, who had looked after his every need for eleven years, had a mental breakdown. And was put into Bethlehem Hospital. Bedlam.

Every day for almost a year the old man asked a servant or friend to conduct him to the outside wall of that sombre building. There they waited. When told that Betsy had waved her handkerchief out of the window he trudged home again. Happy in the knowledge that the bond between them was still intact.

About a year later Betsy recovered, returned home, and married a London optician. She and her husband then cared for Newton, in Colman Buildings, for the rest of his life.

Despite hints from others that he was 'past it', Newton continued to preach.

Richard Cecil, one of the many friends who had enjoyed his ministry for years, was annoyed to see him become so confused in the pulpit. So he put the matter to the old man, rather directly.

"In the article of public preaching, might it not be best to consider your work done?" he enquired, one day.

Newton's response was instant. And adamant. "What !" he almost yelled. "What ! Shall the old African blasphemer stop while he can speak ?"

But he had to stop.

John Newton preached his last sermon in October, 1806. The occasion was a memorial sevice for the victims of the Battle of Trafalgar. It was entirely appropriate, then, that such a gathering shoud be addressed by an ex-sea captain. Someone whom God had called to Himself, and His service, at sea, nearly sixty years before.

At the end of that service, Newton was so weak and confused that he had to be helped from the pulpit.

And he never entered another one.

From early in 1807, John Newton was confined to his room. And soon he was confined to his bed. Betsy devoted herself to caring for him, regulating the steady stream of visitors, who came, still anxious to hear some word of wit or wisdom.

The question the infirm old man was asked most of all, understandably, was, "Well, how are you today?"

Even in his declining days he was never stuck for an answer. Typical replies to enquiries after his health were, "I am packed and sealed and ready for the post", or, "I am like a person going a journey in a stage-coach, who expects its arrival every hour, and is frequently looking out at the window for it."

What calm confidence ! What perfect peace !

On 21st December, 1807, John Newton was extremely weak. Totally worn out. Barely able to speak. A friend at his bedside saw that he was struggling to say something. He leaned over to catch it.

"My memory is almost gone, but I remember two things," he whispered, feebly.

"That I am a great sinner.." He paused to summon up his last breath, before finishing the sentence, "...And that Christ is a great Saviour!"

Then he slipped quietly away. The stage-coach he had been watching for had come. To whisk him off to heaven. To met Christ, the great Saviour. Face to face.

And Mary would be there, too. And William Cowper.

What a meeting ! What a reunion!

What triumph!

Benediction

May the grace of Christ our Saviour
And the Father's boundless love,
With the Holy Spirit's favour,
Rest upon us from above !
Thus may we abide in union
With each other, and the Lord ;
And possess, in sweet communion,
Joys which earth cannot afford.

John Newton.

(Olney Hymns. Book 3. Hymn 101.)

BIBLIOGRAPHY

Cecil, Lord David. **The Stricken Deer. The Life of William Cowper.** Constable, London. 1929.

Edwards, Brian H.. **Through Many Dangers. The story of John Newton.** Evangelical Press. 1975.

Ella, George M.. **William Cowper. Poet of Paradise.** Evangelical Press. 1993.

King, James and Ryskamp, Charles, eds.. **The Letters and Prose Writings of William Cowper.** Clarendon Press. 1979.

Lansdowne Poets, The. **The Poetical Works of William Cowper.** Frederick Warne & Co., London.

Martin, Bernard. **John Newton. A Biography.** William Heinemann Ltd.. 1950.

Milford, H. S., ed.. **Cowper. Poetical Works.** Oxford University Press. 1967.

Newton, John and Cowper, William. **Olney Hymns, in Three Books.** 1st edition, 1779. Bicentenary facsimile edition, published by the trustees of the Cowper and Newton Museum, Olney, Buckinghamshire, England.

Nimmo, William P.. **The Poetical Works of William Cowper.** London. 1876.

Oddy, S. A. **Poems by William Cowper, Esq., of The Inner Temple.** In Two Volumes. London. 1814.

Pollock, John. **Amazing Grace. John Newton's Story.**
Hodder and Stoughton, London. 1981.

Rhodes, Nick, ed.. **William Cowper. Selected Poems.**
Fyfield Books. 1984.

Sambrook, James, ed.. **William Cowper. The Task and Other Selected Poems.** Longman. 1994.

Thomas, Gilbert. **William Cowper and the Eighteenth Century.**
Nicholson & Watson, London. 1935.

Willmott, Rev. Robert A., ed.. **The Poetical Works of William Cowper.** Routledge & Sons, London. 1856.

Wright, Thomas. **The Romance of the Lace Pillow.** New edition.
Ruth Bean. 1982.

INDEX OF HYMNS USED (First Lines)

BOOK 3

Other books by the same author:-

My Father's Hand
This Is For Real
Just The Way I Am
Some Party In Heaven
First Citizen Smith
Something Worth Living For

Acknowledgments

*The publishers would like to thank the past and present
curators of the Cowper and Newton Museum, Olney,
and the present occupants of the Vicarage, Olney, for
their cooperation in the publication of this book.*